Praise for *Headstrong*

"Jones begins her story by taking us through the day of her assault through her own eyes, starting with a seemingly benign walk from the metro station and ending with a savage beating, which we later learn was done with a hammer. She then proceeds to lead us along the roller coaster of her journey of recovery . . . she explores the nature of the new person she has become, learning to navigate her new life, both the good and the bad, managing her losses and celebrating her triumphs: living. As a brain injury survivor, it was a tough read for me. At the same time, I had a lot of trouble putting it down even for brief breaks. *Headstrong* is a page turner and a powerful read."

—DebBrandon, author of *But My Brain Had Other Ideas:*
A Memoir of Recovery from Brain Injury

"*Headstrong* is a book about the trauma resulting from a vicious attack, but it also is a triumphant story of resilience. Jones reveals her intimate and hard-won journey toward recovery. The story is hers to tell—but it is our privilege to see inside the heart of a woman whose life is fortified by love and hope."

—Dr. Patricia Romney, co-editor of *Understanding Power:*
Imperative for Human Services

Headstrong

Headstrong

Surviving
Traumatic Brain Injury

JoAnne Silver Jones

SHE WRITES PRESS

Published 2019
Printed in the United States of America
ISBN: 978-1-63152-612-1
ISBN: 978-1-63152-613-8
Library of Congress Control Number: 2019908829

For information, address:
She Writes Press
1569 Solano Ave #546
Berkeley, CA 94707

She Writes Press is a division of SparkPoint Studio, LLC.

Grateful acknowledgement is made for permission to quote from
The Selected Poems of May Sarton, (Copyright 1971) by W.W.
Norton & Company, Inc.
Washington Post, 2012-04-27 "*Police Search of D.C. Neighborhoods
Leads to Arrest of Assault Suspect*", PARS International Corp.

*To those kindred spirits who live daily with the
consequences and invisibility of traumatic brain injury
and the trauma of random violence*

To Debby

Contents

One: Lamb Shanks

I stepped out of the Metro station and felt a blast of cold air. The inauguration of Barack Obama was only four days away. I was thrilled to be here and thrilled about Barack Obama! As a long-time civil rights activist and professor working toward racial equality, I was elated about the election of our first black president. Eloquent, principled, worldly, and black, he was the bridge between the radical politics of my childhood and my yearning to be hopeful about the future. I was here, in Washington, D.C., to witness, even if from a chilly distance, his swearing in as the forty-fourth President of the United States.

As soon as I ascended the steps of the Metro stop, the frigid wind cut through my multicolored wool sweater, black cashmere cardigan, and red ski jacket. I stopped at the Metro entrance to put on gloves with liners, an ear warmer, and a neck warmer. I was ready for the short walk to my daughter Rachel's house.

Pulling a suitcase, wearing a backpack, and holding a shoulder purse, my body braced against the icy cold that poured through my carefully planned layers. At a little after 7:00 p.m., it was already dark. The sky above was a solid grey, no wispy clouds floating across a starry sky. In the bitter wind, my reverie about the election began to give way to a desire to be warm and with Rachel.

I walked up M Street and then wondered whether to turn right on Eleventh or Tenth. Pulling my rolling suitcase, I imagined I looked like the tourists who walk nervously down Eleventh Street, passing several liquor stores as they head to the hostel a few doors from Rachel's house. At the last minute I decided to turn onto Tenth Street, unaware that this small decision would impact my life, forever bifurcating the years before January 16, 2009 from the years after. I had always enjoyed walking down Tenth Street, lined with majestic three-story brownstones, and tonight, the homes looked especially beautiful, illuminated by soft lights against the backdrop of the dark grey night.

Rachel was bartending at Cork, a wine bar named by the *New York Times* as THE place for Democrats to gather during the inaugural days. Cork was located on Fourteenth Street NW, a street rapidly becoming the "It" place in D.C. It was also an easy walk from her house. Anticipating dinner at Cork, I had eaten very little all afternoon except a cup of black coffee and a chocolate-covered donut from the Dunkin Donuts kiosk at Bradley Airport. I was planning to leave my suitcase and backpack at Rachel's house, clean up a bit, and then walk to Fourteenth Street.

My thoughts shifted to what I would order for dinner. I remembered the menu at Cork from other visits and, in my mind, I glanced through the options, then decided on the lamb shanks cooked in red wine, the kind with the meat falling off the bone. I could almost taste them. Rachel would choose a delicious red wine to pair with the lamb. I could easily imagine sitting on a bar stool, warm and surrounded by the din of conversation, a long-stemmed wine glass filled with Italian red sitting before me. While waiting for my dinner, I would engage in conversation with other customers about who President Obama might choose for his cabinet. We'd share election stories while I delighted in seeing Rachel: I would have to restrain myself from telling everyone, "See that lovely woman, she's my daughter!"

I started to turn left down the alley that abuts Rachel's house. I could see the lights in her living room and I began to feel warmer, just knowing that in a minute or two I would be inside her house. Alleys in this area, lit by streetlights, are wide enough for a vehicle to drive through. It seemed more sensible to take the alley rather than the longer route of going to O Street and having to walk around the block. I felt something hit my head. I thought it might be from a roof. I turned to look up—and my life changed forever.

I saw a man's face inside a hood. Years later, some of the riders on the metro would be clearer in my memory than *his* face. I know it was a man. He was tall. He was African American. He was doing something to me. These were the only images I would recall, and they would remain like a grainy, underdeveloped picture, vague and hard to decipher. I was overwhelmed by terror. I could feel the inside of my body rearranging itself—blood left my feet and raced to my head. I couldn't hear or see. I felt nothing. Terror consumed me; I was only terror. I was being sucked into a void, an abyss without time, place, thoughts, or feelings. Darkness surrounded me and I heard a scream, a sound I'd never heard before, but I didn't know it was coming from me. The sound went on and on, high-pitched wails without volition. Then I was on my back, kicking and keening. My mind flashed to a personal-defense instructor once saying, "Kick a man in the balls." So I kicked wildly. I didn't see anything. I didn't know if my eyes were open or shut. I didn't feel pain; I didn't feel or think anything. I had no conscious sense of fear—fear requires thinking and having a sense of what is happening and what might happen next.

I have no idea how long I was in this world of horror, but I knew I couldn't struggle anymore—my body was slumping. I felt my purse being pulled from my shoulder. The pounding stopped. I sensed I was alone now. I tried to lift my body off the ground and felt excruciating pain in my hands. I saw a hooded shadow running down the alley across the street, holding my purse like a football. I didn't recognize anything around me. I thought I saw a pink house. Panic overtook me. Where was Rachel's house? Where did the pink house come from? Then two women were standing next to me. One said, "Are you cold? Do you need a blanket? Do you need help?"

I responded, "Please take my gloves off." I thought that the pain would stop if only my gloves were off.

Over the years, my understanding of this moment would become clearer: the shadow was running down the alley where I lay, not across the street. The alley did not continue across the street. My limited vision distorted what I saw. There would be no mention in the police report of bystanders. Maybe there really were two women standing next to me, or maybe no one was there. I don't remember being covered with a blanket or touched by anyone. Someone, though, heard me yelling and called 911. That call saved my life.

"Can you tell me your name?" I heard the question and realized that I was in a vehicle, probably an ambulance.

"Do you have my luggage?" I asked.

"Yes, ma'am. We have everything. Can you tell me your name?"

"JoAnne Jones."

"What's your birthday?"

"November 12, 1946. Please call my daughter."

"What's her number?"

From someplace I dredged up her cell phone number. "She's working at Cork now, it's a wine bar on 14th Street. You can just take me to her house. I'm fine."

"I respect your opinions," he replied. "In this case, only my opinion matters. May I cut off your neck warmer?"

Years later, Rachel would tell me that I could not have had this conversation. "You weren't able to speak, Mom. You only made sounds, horrible shrieks." I would never know whether the conversation was audible or happened only in my head. Other than this remnant my memory is blank. For years, though, I would feel panicked by the sound of an ambulance siren.

Two: Memory Shards

I was in the emergency room on a table under very bright lights. I have no memory of the ride to George Washington University Hospital, being brought into the ER, my clothes and jewelry taken off, or any questions being asked. My ER memory starts when Rachel walked in.

"I'm sorry you had to leave your job, honey," I said.

"It's OK, Mom." For an instant I thought I was having a regular interaction, with nothing out of the ordinary happening. I was relieved to see her. Probably about an hour had passed from the time she heard about the assault until she was able to get to the hospital. I didn't know what she was seeing when she looked at me. I didn't know what version of me was on the hospital bed. There were doctors all around, police and police photographers. Lights flashed. More questions. My awareness came and went. "I think it was a brick. I know it wasn't a fist," I said, but I don't recall the question. During my last visit to see Rachel, I had taken some of the dogs boarding with her to a fenced area on Tenth Street. In my mind, I was there again now, dogs playing around me, and I noticed piles of bricks stacked behind the house abutting this little enclosure.

Then I heard the keening sound again. Pain engulfed me. "Mrs. Jones, we need to wrap your hands." Words came and went. I didn't understand. My hands did not constitute an acute medical crisis. The wrapping was a temporary step that involved moving my broken hands into a new position. They were claw-like and needed to be straightened and put in a position perpendicular to my wrists.

Doctors moved my broken hands. The pain was excruciating. I have no idea if I had been given pain medication. My head needed to be stapled immediately and a catheter inserted. I went from being consumed by terror to being consumed by pain. I heard myself bark at the people in the ER. "Please take this neck collar off. I don't need it. It hurts. Please loosen these bandages. My head hurts so much. Just loosen them. Please." Only a world of pain existed. I had no awareness of my condition or what had happened to me. I only wanted the pain to stop.

Early Saturday morning, January 17, Debby, my wife, walked into the ICU. I thought I had smiled and said something like, "I was wondering when you would arrive, honey," as if it were an ordinary day and I had just prepared our dinner. I said it as if I had been patiently waiting to tell her about my adventure the previous evening. At least, I *believed* I had spoken these words out loud, although Debby would report months later that I didn't say anything.

And then all thoughts and memories were blank again. My world was imploding and I now inhabited only an internal space. When I was awake, I rarely opened my eyes.

What I saw in my mind's eye those first few days were images—not like those from dreams, where metaphors replace actual events. They were more like images from a horror movie; the movie might have been fiction but the terror was real and the images lasting. Nothing had a shape. Free-floating amoeba-like things surrounded me. Then nothing. Gray, grainy. Then sudden movement, and the shapes floated and rearranged. I felt so alone, so achingly alone. I was in the midst of nothingness. The images were blurry, jumping around me as they did when I was sixteen and drank a half bottle of vodka and saw the black-and-white bathroom floor swirl around and around.

At some point in those endless hours following the assault, my mind moved from a world of darkness to a world that was all bright and white. I saw a hospital bed in the middle of a room. I was the only person in the room, although occasionally I heard some voices or saw a visitor. I saw brightness, not IV poles; I saw people standing behind me talking softly, sometimes directly to me, although I didn't answer. Scores of doctors and nurses were hovering, asking questions and doing things to me, but I felt only the presence of Debby and a sense of brightness. It wasn't the brightness of joy. The bright was as overwhelming as the dark.

A voice cut through the blur. "We're going to take you into surgery, Mrs. Jones, and clean up your head a bit," Dr. Shields, the neurosurgeon, said to me. "OK," I responded. I didn't really know what he meant. I was a body encased in darkness. I would learn later that he performed a craniotomy about ten hours after the assault.

✶ ✶ ✶

Shard: I see my family from DC standing near me in the white, bright room. They're talking but I'm not saying anything and I can't hear what they're saying.

Shard: The officer who found me in the alley is standing near me. She introduces me to someone. "This is my partner on the job and my partner in life." I don't understand what she's saying. I don't respond.

Shard: Three days after surgery, on Inauguration Day, I leave the ICU for a surgical room. I am wheeled down a hall on a hospital bed thinking, "So this is where I am. I'm in a hospital."

One eye can open now, and I can see around me. The new room is small and dark and filled with flowers. News of the assault has spread through my circle of family and friends and has been picked up by the local media. Flowers pour into the hospital. They were not permitted in ICU, but now I'm surrounded by flower arrangements.

Shard: A nurse removes the urinary catheter and says in an even tone, "Please eat something, Mrs. Jones. You've been receiving nourishment and liquid by IVs for four days and now you need to eat on your own." I feel embarrassed. I've been letting tubes take care of me. I can't imagine eating.

Shard: More flowers arrive. People come in and out to say *hello* and *how are you.* I don't know the answer.

Shard: I have to pee. My arms and hands are bandaged. I can only see out of one eye and can't look up without getting very dizzy. I tell a nurse that I have to pee. She escorts me and my IV pole to the bathroom. She leaves. I manage to sit down. When she comes back I find the energy to tell her that I can't clean myself. "Oh," she says. She leaves and comes back with what I think is a bath towel. She cleans me. I am humiliated. I feel overwhelming fatigue.

Shard: Rachel comes into the small, dark post-surgical hospital room. She asks if I want her to brush my teeth. Our roles are now reversed. She is taking care of me, thinking about what I need and helping me. It's been five days since I brushed my teeth. Gratefully, I nod. She helps me to sit on the bed. I open my mouth and she gently and slowly brushes my teeth. The toothpaste feels reviving, like quenching a thirst I didn't know I had. Rachel hands me a glass of water and holds it to my lips so I can rinse my mouth in the bowl she holds in front of me.

Thank you, honey.

She smiles.

Shard: I want to see Michelle Obama's inaugural gown. The TV is attached high on the wall across from my bed. I can't look up without getting dizzy. When the TV commentators announce the arrival of the first couple, with great effort I look up at the TV. I can look for only a few minutes at her white, off-the-shoulder gown. I'm exhausted. I lower my eyes and fall asleep.

***

Now I was wearing the uniform of the patient: loose-fitting, thin cotton, and open so that all parts of my body were accessible for examination. I was clothed in a garment of vulnerability. I completely inhabited the role of patient.

By day five, I was more aware of the contingent of doctors and medical students who began their rounds at 5:00 a.m. Teams of trauma doctors, orthopedists, and neurosurgeons visited me. Each team walked in en masse, and then took up position at the end of my bed. No questions were off limits.

Can you move your arm? Can you move your leg? What day is it? What is your birthday? Did you urinate today? Did you move your bowels? What did you eat? What is your pain on a scale of one to ten? May I touch you here? And here? And here?

My job was to answer.

Thank you, Mrs. Jones.

They left quickly.

George Washington University Hospital was my new home. Not a home in the sense that I made decisions, or felt ownership, or knew anything beyond the door to my room. But it was my entire world. I recognized the sound of the blood-pressure cart, the particular shuffle of the trauma team in contrast to the rapid click of the neurology team. There were always medical students with the trauma team. They made more noise and asked more questions. Dr. Shields's visits were quicker and he sometimes came without an entourage. I was able to tell time by the sounds around me. The morning food cart and smell of weak coffee meant early morning. Doctors visited in the morning. Lights were dimmed in the evening, although the sounds never stopped. Cleaning staff moved quietly through the room after the evening meal was served.

I learned the names of the nurses who took care of me, and came to know their shift times. I was more eager to see certain nurses than others. Some of the nurses spoke to me directly and in soft, comforting tones. They smiled. They asked what they could do to make me more comfortable. I asked my favorite nurses some questions about themselves. Occasionally they asked a question about my life before I inhabited a hospital bed. I could report facts: *I am a college professor. My hometown is San Francisco. I live with my wife in Amherst, Massachusetts. My daughter lives in D.C.* But I could barely remember my life before the assault. My palpable reality was the safety of my bed, the world within the walls of the hospital, and the floating sensation that came every four hours from morphine. I knew the orderlies and the cleaning staff and the medical students and the auxiliary staff. We were all part of the same home.

I was learning a new language: CT scan, MRI, TBI, PTs, OTs, trauma teams, neurosurgery teams, ophthalmology teams, orthopedic teams. These teams came and they went. Asked more questions. I often couldn't follow their questions, but I tried to respond. The occupational therapist (OT) came in and tried to rig up a way for me to hold a spoon with my bandaged hands. I was grateful for her attention, but using my hands in any way was impossible.

Often a comment was made about what had happened to me. The ophthalmologist was almost in tears. "What kind of person would do this?" he asked in a tremulous voice. Some nurses and orderlies apologized on behalf of D.C. "I'm so sorry this happened to you here in D.C." I didn't really know what had happened to me. I felt numb and weary.

There were a few people—one orderly and one member of the police department—who probed and asked, "Did you fight him?" "Did you just give him your purse?"

"Well, I fought. He didn't ask for my purse," I answered very concretely.

"Thought so. Usually it's the tourists who fight back," they said. In my mind these men in uniform were now one person. Fear surged through my body.

People who fight back get hurt. They implied that the injuries were my fault. I started to wonder.

✶ ✶ ✶

Shard: I don't know or understand my medical condition. I have headaches and bandages around my head. My hands hurt all the time. My health needs are tended to and there are some doctors who reach beyond my injuries into my wounded spirit. One doctor, before beginning a procedure, leans over and whispers in my ear, "Try to find a Zen place." When he says these words, I relax and let myself float beyond the procedure. His words offer a way to find myself that is beyond pain, beyond fear, and untouched by violence. These words will become a guiding beacon, an important way that I'll learn to deal with the myriad medical procedures and issues I still have to face.

I still inhabit a netherworld. I feel as though I am ensconced in a mesh net. I can now see and sense and hear more, but I continue to be restrained by barriers I can't understand. I cannot often enough find that place where my muscles relax and my mind calms, and where I'm not protecting myself from something unknown.

Three: Rachel, Debby, and Trauma's Long Reach

The only calling I've had in my life is the desire to be a mother. I wanted a child to look at me while standing at the top of a slide and yell, "Mommy, watch me." I've loved all of the pieces of mothering.

I married Mike, Rachel's father, when I was twenty years old. It was the Vietnam era, and in the zeitgeist of that time young men were deciding what do to when they received a 1A, fit for duty, military draft classification. During the 1960s and early 70s, receiving a 1A likely meant a tour of duty in Vietnam. Mike and I were so young and so different from each other. My grandparents had fled from pogroms, Jewish ghettos in Russia, into the Jewish diaspora, leaving behind their Yiddish shtetl names and history. Mike, on the other hand, could trace his heritage back to the Mayflower and Davey Crockett. We made the romantic, marry-before-he-goes-to war decision when his "orders came for sailing somewhere over there." Unlike Lili Marleen, I wasn't standing under a lamplight, but sobbing and waving farewell as he stood on the deck of the aircraft carrier, the USS Constellation. I was a junior in college and my man was off to a war that he thought was just and that I loathed.

He served two tours of duty in Vietnam while I finished my undergraduate degree and began a masters of social work degree. Marriage was a mystery, and we spent our first years separated by distance and politics. My desire to be a mother remained strong. After Vietnam, he was transferred to the naval base on Kodiak Island, Alaska, and when his naval service ended, we moved south to Calgary, Alberta. Rachel was born in Canada.

When she was two, we divorced. He was a mountain man, at home in the wilderness, less so in the company of urban folk. After the divorce, he moved to the far north of British Columbia on the Stewart-Cassiar Highway, one of only two roads that connect Canada to Alaska. He took people on hunting and fishing expeditions, sold gasoline, food, and lodging, and for two months each winter he ran a trap line in an even more remote location. His winter income came from the pelts he sold.

Just before Christmas of 1990, we received a phone call telling us that Mike did not meet the small plane scheduled to ferry him back to his home. The pilot did find Mike's dog, Chinook, alone and emaciated. Mike was presumed dead. Everyone knew that he would never leave his dog.

In the spring of 1991, when the snow and ice melted, his body and the snowmobile he'd been riding were found. He was forty-seven. Rachel was fourteen. She asked me to promise that I would not die until she was at least eighteen and could take care of herself. Like her father, she handled life's assaults stoically, managing the ensuing practical consequences with aplomb and submerging the emotional costs.

* * *

The night of my assault, she was bartending at Cork. She never answered her phone while working. The police finally called the restaurant directly and spoke to the hostess. The message passed along to Rachel was simply that her mom was in the hospital and wanted to see her. It didn't seem like an emergency.

She left work and began to listen to her voice messages. The picture quickly changed. There were many calls from the police, each saying that I had been severely injured and asking her to come immediately to the ER at George Washington University Hospital. Because so many roads were closed in preparation for the inauguration, a trip that normally took ten minutes took over thirty. She didn't know what had happened or the condition of her mother.

Rachel told me later that when she got to the ER I was making sounds, but the only words she heard me say were, "Please stay." She stayed with me in the emergency room most of the night and, other than work she had to do, remained at the hospital until I was released.

She also told me that the police found my cell phone near me in the alley. They called the last number I had dialed and reached Debby. "You weren't able to speak, Mom. You only made sounds, horrible shrieks."

I am ashamed to admit that years passed before I was able to take in the powerful impact of the assault on those closest to me.

∗ ∗ ∗

Debby is a tall, striking woman. Her height and the sheen of her salt-and-pepper hair, coupled with a ready laugh and exuberant curiosity about people, make her stand out in a room. She's like a full-spectrum light bulb, illuminating spaces that guide others out of their malaise.

Debby and I met when we were both adults and single parents to only children. Rachel was in her senior year of high school and Debby's son Robbie was a sophomore in the same high school. We both had professional careers and wide circles of friends and family. We had both been in long-term relationships and a few brief ones. Our lives were settled. We met at the birthday party of a mutual friend, and at the end of the party Debby asked me for a ride home. During the car ride, she said something funny and I couldn't stop laughing. It was the kind of soul-cleansing laugh, where all senses are focused on being fully alive in the moment.

The next day we made plans to meet for dinner, and as we slowly picked away at an order of sushi and California rolls and sipped a single glass of sake, we told our respective life stories.

She began: "I live with trauma. I have a lot of PTSD. Most people don't know that about me." She told me that, along with her mother and older brother and sister, she spent every summer on Martha's Vineyard. Her father would continue working and then join the family for parts of the summer. "It was a magical place," she said. "Still is. Before starting seventh grade my mother decided to take me on a special weekend to the Vineyard, just the two of us. It was late August, just after I turned twelve. She rented a little cottage in the village of Menemsha. I can't remember how I felt about spending this time just with her. I guess at that age I didn't think about her that much. I had my own worries, like being tall and going into seventh grade. Early on our first morning, I heard my mother make a sound. We were in the same bed. I woke up and knew something was wrong. She didn't seem to be breathing. I was terrified. I ran out of the cottage and down the hill to a nearby house. I was screaming and banging on the door. Someone called an ambulance and called my father. She was dead. My mother was dead. I still wonder if I ran fast enough. Did I linger in the cottage before running for help? Did I bang loud enough when I got to the house?" Debby said she shut down that day, and that now she was always afraid someone she loved would die or get sick. "I always have to remain vigilant," she told me.

Forty years later, on the evening of January 16, 2009, she was at a birthday party in Holyoke, Massachusetts, about a twenty-five-minute drive from our home in Amherst, when her cell phone rang and the caller said, "Do you know JoAnne Jones?"

"Yes."

"What is your name? How do you know JoAnne Jones?"

"She's my wife."

"Oh. Sit down. I have something to tell you. She's been badly injured. We found her phone and your number was the last one she called."

Debby listened, wrote down the information, and called Rachel and our cousin Lisa who lives in D.C. Realizing that she was barely able to think, let alone make plane reservations, she called our friends Arlene and Martha, told them what happened, and asked for their help. She went to their home, where they handled all of the logistical arrangements for her trip to D.C. Another friend took her to the airport for her 6:00 a.m. flight to Washington.

Four: Awake

On day seven I was moved to a new room. The head nurse had said I should be in the best room on the floor. Once again the bed, with me as passenger, was moved along with dozens of bouquets of flowers. The new room was bright, with floor-to-ceiling windows along one side overlooking Pennsylvania Avenue, the path of the inaugural parade now three days past. There was also a view of the Washington Monument. At one point I actually sat in a chair and looked out the window. I could now stay awake for longer periods and talked to many of the staff members who came and went, and to my family and friends who never left my side. I looked out at the Washington Monument, cars moving through the streets, ever-present construction happening nearby, and all I wanted was to return to my hospital bed, the world I now occupied. On the bed, I felt separate and protected from everyday life; I had no responsibilities and, with the help of morphine, no memories or pain.

Two close friends from home were now part of my daily hospital life. Before I moved to my big room Debby had told me, "Pat called. She's taking the train down. She'll be here Thursday and Linda is flying through D.C. on her way home from Seattle. She'll spend the weekend here."

"Hey Jo." Pat, who doesn't drink coffee, handed me a large cup of Starbucks. "You like your coffee black and hot, right? Just like your mother? If this coffee was as hot as she liked it, the straw would melt." She laughed and held the straw to my lips. She brought me life beyond the hospital room in an effortless, matter-of-fact way. "Do you want a bagel? We bought some with cream cheese," Linda added. "We'll get you whatever you want."

I heard the patter of their conversation: "It's like a winter carnival outside. There are vendors everywhere selling whatever they can put the name *Obama* on; some people are wearing costumes and music is blaring."

Debby walked in and added, "I think I saw a famous person leaving a fancy restaurant. You know her. She was married to what's-his-name. And she was wearing a full-length mink coat . . ."

"The sidewalks are still so crowded even though the inauguration is over," Linda said.

We didn't talk about test results or medical issues. Linda and Pat stepped into our new daily routines, offered Rachel and Debby needed breaks from the hospital, and provided a glimpse of the event that brought me to Washington.

As I became more awake, I began to dream. On my first night in the new room, HE came into my room. Rather, IT hovered at the door, tall and hooded but without a body. Attached to the hood was something that looked like a cape, billowing and blocking the door. I thought IT was coming towards me. I screamed, though the sound was inside of me. Then IT receded, lurking at the edges of my awakening consciousness. In the morning I told Debby, who was now sleeping in my room, wedged on a small sofa with her legs on a chair. She told me that she hadn't heard me make any sounds during the night.

Over the ensuing years, she occasionally would hear me screaming in my sleep. I wouldn't hear myself making sounds during the night, but would continue to catch glimpses of a cape, just at the margins of my peripheral vision.

* * *

In the hospital, I could do nothing for myself. When awake, I often searched for the Zen place—the place of calm that helped me to deal with the reality of my condition. I felt guided by my father in my search for this place and in the practice of gratitude. At times, as I lay in the hospital bed, I could sense my father in me. He was a stoic and patient man: during the last years of his life he labored through a neurological disease that affected all of his muscle functions. By the end of his life, he could no longer blink, raise a finger, or express himself in any ordinary way. Yet he exuded a kind of calm. He fought the disease as hard and as long as he could, but his fight was never at the expense of others: he made powerful connections with others until the end of his life. I don't know what thoughts went through his mind as his body hardened, but I know that I felt a sense of tranquility when I was with him. And now, during the painful and debilitating weeks following my assault, I felt my father's tranquility and he quelled my terror. He filled me with his love. He gave me a thread to hold on to.

I was also inspired by my friend Leah, who fought leukemia for as long as she could. In her last bout, at age forty-four, she underwent a bone marrow transplant. Following the transplant, she had to stay in a room isolated from others and wait for her body to signal that she was strong enough to join the world beyond her hospital room. I spent five days in this secluded room with her. Her bed was centered in the middle of the room, bordered by IV poles. She only had the strength to move in order to use the portable toilet next to the bed. Yet with all of this, Leah still responded to others as if they were guests invited into her home. She was gracious and thoughtful. She said *thank you* to each person who entered, whether their job was to sweep the floor or give her blood test results. While ensconced in her own world of struggle, she was so kind to others. I felt her speak to me now as throngs of people came and went from my hospital room. *Thank you. Please. That's so kind of you. May I.* She gave me a way to be in this unimaginable situation. Like my father, she also gave me a thread to hold on to.

Many people came in and out of my room. In addition to hospital staff, members of the D.C. police department, particularly those from the Victims Assistance Unit, visited and talked about the services they could offer. The room was bustling while I lay in bed clad in the hospital johnnie, wondering what was being discussed. I remained entrenched in my own miasma.

* * *

On Friday morning, January 23, Debby was sitting next to me. Her phone rang and I heard her say, "JoAnne's purse?" I tried to pay attention. *Who is calling? What's happening?* Debby only said that my purse had been located and mentioned the name of the person who called.

"Where? Where was it found?"

"In the parking lot of the Giant supermarket," she said.

I knew the neighborhood. The Giant was only two blocks from Rachel's house and bordered a historic part of D.C. Before my life changed, when visiting Rachel, I would sometimes walk there to get the morning paper. I loved meandering through the alleys of Naylor Court with signs saying "horse shoeing" and "board your horse" still clearly visible along the wide, cobble-stoned roads, built before the White House was constructed. These old buildings, once home to a thriving African American community, were now filled with upscale condos and restaurants but still reflected the architecture of the nineteenth and early twentieth centuries.

I could barely follow the story about where my purse was found, who found it, and who was bringing it to the hospital. I fell asleep.

I heard loud voices. Debby had gone to the hospital lobby to retrieve the paper bag that held my purse, and as she walked into my room, she gave the bag to Linda. No one wanted me to see the bag or the purse. Linda took the bag into the bathroom. I didn't see her opening the purse and finding a bloody hammer.

I don't know what Linda thought or felt at that moment. I don't remember much. There was a flurry of activity and tension filled the room. I heard Debby calling the police. In a rapid, anxious voice she said that a hammer was found in my purse; found in the Giant parking lot; given to a security officer; brought to the hospital. *We have it. There's a hammer in the purse. There is dried blood all over the hammer.*

I was in and out of sleep or maybe consciousness. I heard, and didn't hear. Understood a little bit, but not the magnitude of finding a bloody hammer, a hammer with my blood caked on it.

At some point a police officer came to take custody of the hammer. I don't know his name. I don't remember if he was wearing a uniform or if he ever introduced himself to me. My only *feeling* memory is that he didn't seem that interested in what, for everyone else in the room, was a traumatic event, a significant find.

I remained in bed, covered with a thin blanket and connected to IV poles. He held a digital camera and began the autopsy of my purse.

Mrs. Jones (they all call me Mrs. Jones): Is this your brush? *Yes.* Click.

Is this your checkbook? *Yes.* Click.

Is this your lip gloss? *Yes.* Click.

Is this your glasses case? *Yes.* Click.

Are these your glasses? *Yes.* Click.

Are these your lipsticks? *Yes.* Click.

I felt embarrassed. He took out crumpled tissues and, to my great relief, didn't ask me to claim them as my own.

He pulled out a bank envelope and began to count the money inside. "Four hundred dollars in twenty-dollar bills. Is this yours?" I began to justify why I had this money. "I went to the bank just before

I left home because I was worried that I wouldn't have enough money. Yes. It's mine."

Click.

He pulled out another envelope and put the contents on the autopsy table.

"Can you tell me what this is and if it's yours?"

Swallowing, I said that they were Israeli shekels that belonged to my stepfather. I thought my daughter . . .

"Are they yours?" he interrupted.

"Yes." Click.

He paused and put everything back in the purse. "You can keep the purse." He began to hand me the purse. Debby grabbed it before it touched me.

"Will you be able to get fingerprints from the hammer?" someone asked.

"That only happens on TV, not in real life. This isn't *CSI*," he answered derisively. "We don't even get fingerprints from a gun."

His job was done. He left.

I receded back into myself.

It would be three years before I could emotionally revisit this moment, and then I was filled with questions: did he put the hammer in a plastic bag and label the bag like they do on *Law and Order*? Did he wear gloves to handle everything? He took pictures, but did he label anything he saw? Did he call the Giant supermarket for more information? Did anyone ever look at his report? Where was it logged? Was a DNA test ever done?

With the discovery of the hammer, I understood that the hooded shadow beat me with a hammer. It was knowledge that would take years to wend itself to a realization: the strength and power of a hammer as a weapon; the vitriol necessary to swing such a weapon at another person. At the time, the discovery served as the answer to the question, "What happened?"

I never saw *that* hammer, but the sight of any hammer will always make me sick.

* * *

Later that same day, a hospital social worker came to my room to discuss discharge plans. She said that the physical and occupational therapy staff weren't available on weekends, and so I would be discharged later in the day. I could, she noted, continue my rehabilitation at Rachel's home in D.C. and then in Amherst when I return. I was confused. OT and PT were so unimportant at this point. My hands and arms were completely bandaged and broken. I was in constant pain. I could barely stand without getting dizzy. My head was stapled and bandaged. I didn't need occupational therapy. I didn't need physical therapy. I needed safety.

The social worker spoke in a cold, detached way, as if she were delivering hospital policy to a mannequin. It was hard for me to understand what she was saying. I wanted her out of my room.

"I can't go," I said to Debby, pleading with her to save me.

My advocacy crew—Debby, Pat, and Linda—immediately went into action. They consulted with my primary-care physician, and talked to the social worker again and to the head of the trauma team. Within an hour or two, a decision was made to let me stay in the hospital over the weekend and leave on Monday.

* * *

During this first week in the hospital I had no reason or desire to look in a mirror. What thoughts I had were focused on sleep and pain relief. On the Saturday before I was to be discharged, eight days after the assault, I decided to look in the mirror.

My hospital room was quieter than usual that day. I was alone and finally able to get out of bed on my own. Linda and Pat had returned home earlier in the day, and Rachel and Debby were doing something on their own. I was by myself, and lucid. I wondered, "What do I look like?"

I got out of bed and walked to the bathroom. I was no longer tethered to a pole. Even though I was in a private room, the bathroom was hospital standard: small, space only for a toilet and sink. The walls, floor, and fixtures were all a dull white color. Until this particular Saturday, every time I'd passed the mirror, I had turned my head and looked in the opposite direction, or just closed my eyes and stepped forward. I couldn't bear to look. This time I turned toward the mirror.

I knew I'd be shocked, but I wasn't prepared for what I saw. When I didn't know what I looked like, I had imagined myself as injured, but not mangled. I had pictured a scene in *Law and Order: Special Victims Unit*, when Benson and Stabler visit the victim in hospital. She is bandaged and bruised and struggles to speak, but she is not odd or weird-looking.

I glanced at the mirror, and the reflection it returned was of a woman with a thin, drawn face. Her hair was shaved right above her forehead. Her eyes were swollen. She wore what looked like a headband, and behind the headband was a kind of Mohawk-style hairdo with tufts of maroon-colored hair standing straight up. I didn't recognize this person; I didn't want her to be me. The headband, I suddenly realized, was actually the row of stitches holding together the parts of my scalp opened for the craniotomy. The maroon Mohawk was dried blood from the assault and the surgery.

I didn't see *me*. I saw someone fragile, someone whose complexion was the color of the bathroom, drawn and washed out. When I tried to put together that image with the reality that *I* was that face in the mirror, the magnitude of the assault overwhelmed me. I returned to the safety of my hospital bed.

There was no place to bathe and I couldn't get my hands or my whole head wet. I couldn't use my hands at all. I asked a nurse to help me at least to get some of the dried blood out of my hair. In the small bathroom, she took my johnnie off and I sat on a chair with my back facing the sink. She took a towel and gently daubed at my scalp. The towel quickly turned a dark brown. She repeated this for about fifteen minutes and then helped me into clean hospital garb. My thumbs were not wrapped in gauze so I could still use them to feel and touch. I put my thumbs to my damp, matted, still-bloody hair. My stomach tightened and my head began to throb. I saw the image in the mirror—one I didn't want to believe was me. I was sickened from touching clumps of caked blood. I felt dirty and ugly, and began to grasp the enormity of what had happened.

Five: The Return

I was discharged from George Washington University Hospital on January 26, 2009. Rachel brought my cashmere navy-blue sweater, jeans, underwear, and boots and helped me dress. Even though I'd lost weight, the button on the jeans wouldn't close. My stomach was distended from the medication I took to help my bowels move, the medication to stop nausea, the medication to stop pain, to stop infection, to increase iron levels, to lift my mood. She pulled the bottom of the sweater over the jean snap and a nurse helped me into a wheelchair.

Rachel left the room to retrieve the personal items I had been wearing during the assault, which were held in the hospital safe. She returned with a plastic garbage bag containing the jewelry I was wearing—my wedding ring, my watch, and my grandmother's diamond ring that she bought on lay-away, putting in a few dollars every week for two years. Another plastic bag contained my blood-soaked clothes.

A nurse pushed the wheelchair, and Debby walked beside me as I said goodbye to the nurses and orderlies on duty at that time. I felt like I was leaving home.

For the first time in ten days, I was outside. It was another cold, gray day. I shuddered with memories of the cold air on the night of the assault. Rachel and Debby carefully helped me into the back seat of Rachel's car. Everything seemed strange: wearing clothes, seeing people walk and drive, being out of bed. I could feel the motion of the car and as I looked out the window, I felt grateful to have a barrier between me and the bustle and noise of the streets.

A snowstorm was predicted for Wednesday, the day we planned to leave. Some people advised me not to go to Rachel's house at all and to return home immediately. The advice of others was to stay at Rachel's house until the storm passed. I ached to go to Rachel's house for a few days. I felt like I hadn't seen her or been with her as I always did when I visited D.C. I had to be with her outside of the hospital setting. But I also needed to leave for home by Wednesday in order to see my primary-care doctor and to get an appointment with an orthopedic surgeon. I was determined to go to Rachel's house and determined to leave for Massachusetts on Wednesday.

In retrospect, I see my resolve at the end of my hospital stay to see Rachel and to leave for home during a snowstorm as a sign of grit, endurance in a difficult situation and continuing on without complaint. It was my first step away from being a victim toward exercising some control; I couldn't do anything for myself and was conscious only for brief periods of time. During those times when I was awake, I was pummeled with constant headaches, sharp pains in my head, severe pain in both hands, and never-ending dizziness, but I was determined to shape my own life within the limits of the possibilities available.

I was exhausted from the effort of getting dressed, leaving the hospital, and the ride to Rachel's. All I wanted to do was sleep. Rachel gave her bedroom to Debby and me, taking the office/guest room for herself. She helped me up the stairs, took my boots off. I lay down and in seconds was asleep.

When I woke up, I needed to go to the bathroom. I called Debby, and she helped me get to the bathroom, cleaned me, and helped me get downstairs. Rachel's friend Helen brought over homemade lasagna for our dinner. I was learning, again and again, that people want to do something, anything, to help during a difficult time. Helen was gracious and engaging. "Lasagna is the only food I know how to make. I wanted to do something, though," she said with a genuine laugh. Debby fed me. I was too tired to be self-conscious about how I looked or about being fed.

The next day, Debby went to visit her niece and I returned to my usual spot in the corner of the sofa. Rachel fed me, took me to the toilet, and in the afternoon we watched the original version of *Death at a Funeral*. It is a zany film and for a while I was caught up in the film's silly antics.

My hair was still caked with blood and I had not bathed in over ten days. Rachel offered to bathe me and I gladly accepted. Had I been more present within myself, I would have been more reticent to be bathed by my daughter. Rachel's even manner helped me to push past my own awkwardness. We went upstairs together, and I climbed the stairs slowly, my elbow touching the wall for balance. She helped me undress and then gently wrapped my bandaged arms in Saran Wrap to keep them dry. She supported me as I stepped into the tub. The warm water felt so soothing. She held my head as my body slid into the warm water. I felt comforted, my whole body unclenching as the water surrounded me. She used a shower nozzle attached to a hose to wash my body with soap and warm water. I tilted my head back as she carefully rinsed the blood out of my hair, mindful not to touch the row of stitches circumnavigating my skull. She shampooed and gently massaged my scalp, rinsing away more blood, hospital smells, and gravel from the alley. Soon the water ran clear. She helped me out of the tub and tenderly dried me with the brown Nat Berkus bath towel we bought together when she first moved into her house. She dressed me in a pair of flannel pajama bottoms and a shirt with three-quarter-length sleeves that once belonged to my mother.

"I wish you didn't have to do this for me," I said in a hushed tone.

"If I had to do this for the rest of my life, it would be my honor, Mom," Rachel responded in her clear, firm voice.

This moment is forever stored in a deep part of my heart.

* * *

On Wednesday I was unwavering in my decision to leave for Amherst. My dear friends Sheila and Kevin had called me days earlier from their home in Calgary, Alberta to say casually, as if it were an everyday occurrence, that they had hired a medical transporter to take me from D.C. to Amherst. "It's far too expensive. I can take a train," I said adamantly. Kevin commented, with his customary dry wit, "It's really a favor to us. We're using this special fund set up by Ethel [a mutual acquaintance, now deceased, who was uncomfortable with my Jewishness] and we need to spend it soon. This really isn't for you. And think of what Ethel's reaction would be when we spend her money on you," he joked. I accepted reluctantly. Now I realize that, without the medical transport, I don't know how I could have made this long trip.

At 7:30 a.m. on Wednesday, January 28, 2009, a van with two attendants arrived. They were cheerful and upbeat in spite of the falling snow and ice coating the steps to Rachel's house. They talked about the best way to get me into the van. I was dressed in the same clothes I'd slept in and Rachel's heavy wool shirt. It is always hard for me to say goodbye to Rachel after a visit, but this time was far worse. I wanted to stay and take care of her in the wake of this devastating event, and I wanted to let her take care of me. I was bereft.

With tears streaming down my face, I was hoisted into the van. In the back were a hospital bed and a regular van seat. They adjusted my body so that I could lie comfortably, and then arranged pillows under each arm. My fleece-lined knee-high boots were pulled off and the wool jacket taken gently off my shoulders. The luggage was loaded in the back and Debby sat in the seat next to me. Rachel bravely waved goodbye.

The van drove down Eleventh Street and turned left onto M Street. At the intersection of M and Tenth, I tried to roll back the tape in my mind and imagined walking up Eleventh Street instead of Tenth on January 16. I wanted to make a different choice, to rearrange the past; I wanted to bargain with Time and make this nightmare disappear. During the years that followed, I would learn that my focus on changing fate or happenstance—making the random knowable—is a common reaction in victims of violence. It is both an effort to retroactively change the outcome of a horrible event and a belief that the victim bears culpability for whatever happened. Each decision prior to the traumatic event is scrutinized through the lens of "if only." For me it was, "If only I didn't stop to put on more layers; if only I was more vigilant as I walked; if only I had paid attention to all the people near me; if only . . . if only . . ."

The Convention Center and metro stop were at the corner of Tenth Street and Eighth Avenue, where the van now stopped for a red light and then turned away from the sights that elicited "if only." I refocused my gaze inside the van and saw a note attached to the back of the driver's seat. *YES WE CAN,* it proclaimed. I smiled. This was Sheila, with her brilliant sense of timing and humor, reaching through miles and misery to offer the perfect message. The van was also stocked with our favorite foods: yogurt, fruit, candy bars, potato chips, juice, and water, all organized by Sheila to make this difficult trip as comfortable as possible.

The ride from D.C. to Amherst took nine hours rather than the usual seven because of weather conditions. I stared out the window most of that time. I didn't eat or talk. I didn't think about the past days or anything else in particular. Occasionally I heard snippets of conversation in the van.

"Where are you from?" Debby asked the attendants as the trip began. She is always curious about people.

"Georgia," they answered in unison.

"Wow. You're already a long way from home. What are your names?"

"I'm Pamela and this is LeRoy, driving. I'm also an EMT . . . What happened?" Pamela asked tentatively.

I heard only a few words.

"Hammer . . . titanium plates and mesh . . . both hands . . . No, didn't catch him."

The sound of inhaled shock.

✳ ✳ ✳

Debby spent most of the drive trying to find a surgeon to operate on my hands. I heard her making one call after another. I knew she was doing this for me, but I also wanted her to stop talking. I didn't want any more sounds or voices. She continued because the orthopedic team had said my hands were getting "sticky" and should be operated on as soon as I was home.

Sticky. "The property of adhering." Adhering to what? What is sticky?

At that time, all I knew was that sticky meant something had to be done soon. Years later I came to understand that sticky referred to the growth of soft tissue, called osseous, that forms following a fracture and immediately begins to unite the shattered fragments. This tissue soon becomes callused, solidifying the fractured pieces into a hardened position.

✳ ✳ ✳

When she was ten, Rachel made the long trek by herself to visit her father at Tatoga Lake in northern British Columbia. We were living in Calgary at the time. It was a very long trip for a ten-year-old child. Two days after she arrived at Tatoga Lake, Mike called me. "I have good news and bad news," he said in his deep, slow, country voice. "The good news is that Rachel is going to be fine. The bad news is that she was in a snowmobile accident and her nose is pretty busted up."

He took her immediately to the closest doctor, an hour-and-a-half drive along country roads. According to Rachel, the doctor was nonplussed by her late-night arrival. He admonished her to be more careful, cleaned her up, and stitched up the loosely hanging skin flaps of her nose. When I picked her up at the Calgary airport a week later, I was shocked by her appearance. Her face was swollen and her nose was misshapen. She looked like Miss Piggy. She smiled and hugged me. I hugged her and said nothing about her appearance. We were both trying to be brave. At that time in my life, brave still meant saying nothing and moving on.

At my friend Yael's urging, I took Rachel to see the best plastic surgeon in Calgary. As soon as he saw Rachel, he said that she needed immediate surgery. "She should have been airlifted to Vancouver for surgery right after the accident. She is a healthy child and her nose is *sticky*. Soon surgery will be impossible. She'll need reconstructive surgery." I didn't ask him what "sticky" actually meant, but I never forgot that it meant *urgent*. The following day he operated, taking cartilage from her ribs to reconstruct the tip of her nose.

✶ ✶ ✶

After a few hours of calling orthopedic practices, Debby called Pat, knowing that Pat had connections with some local hospitals. Pat offered the name of a colleague and friend who was the vice president of a nearby hospital. Debby contacted him immediately and he called right back, saying that he highly recommended Dr. David Refermat, a surgeon in the plastic surgery department. One call to Dr. Refermat and I had an appointment on Friday, January 30.

I gazed out the window of the van, eyes looking outward but

seeing only a blur. My inward vision was a blur as well. I was aware only of the movement of the van, not of time or a place. Every few hours we stopped. LeRoy and Pamela would remove the pillows holding up my arms, put on my boots and my wool shirt, and help me out of the van. Debby would take me to the bathroom. In New York we stopped at what LeRoy said was his favorite road restaurant. "The burgers are great and so is the chicken sandwich. Can I get you something, JoAnne? Do you want a Coke?" he said in a voice so kind, I began to cry.

"No, thank you." I didn't want anything. I just wanted to go back to a bed and be alone with my emptiness.

After nine hours, the medical transport pulled up our frozen driveway. I saw our friend Martha, arms outstretched toward me, walk out of our front door. "We've got her. Thanks," LeRoy said. These amazing people, who had insured my safe return, who'd made a long and dangerous trip seem like a road trip, now brought me into my house and helped me to the white denim slipcovered sofa. For the last time, they pulled off my boots and gently removed the wool shirt.

"I don't know how to thank you," I said, tears welling up in my eyes.

"Just get well. That's all we want," Pamela said tenderly. They reached down and gently hugged me.

I had no idea how treacherous the next months would be. I couldn't have imagined yet another major health crisis as a result of the assault, or events that would further galvanize my traumatic reactions, or the betrayals I would endure.

Six: Apples and Trees

As I try to put the assault and the ways in which it has changed the landscape of my life into context, I think about my childhood and my cultural and emotional inheritance. I can see how these roots have shaped my responses and have been key to my rebuilding efforts.

My mother tells the story of her childhood as the combination of deprivation and triumph. The oldest of seven children born to Russian immigrants, her early memories are of being hungry, taking care of one baby after another, and moving one step ahead of an eviction notice. She delighted in telling the story about when she was six and rode on the back of ice delivery trucks for fun. One day, a block of ice fell on her head. Undaunted, she got herself up and caught the next ice truck! It was the getting up, not the falling down, that she emphasized.

She was the protector and tormentor of her younger siblings. She took care of them as well as ordered them around. And, she would add, anyone who called her or one of her siblings a "dirty Jew" was summarily beaten and advised never to repeat that remark again. One of her fondest childhood memories was of the time her mother was hospitalized for a year after a spleen operation. There were five children in the family then. My grandfather couldn't be expected to care for his children, so my mother and three siblings were sent to an orphanage: The Jewish Home for Orphans and Waifs in Worcester, Massachusetts. She loved it! She had a bed to herself, food to eat, and the rooms were warm. "It was heaven," she always said. Her youngest sibling, then six months old, was taken in a by a family with twelve children. The family saw no problem with taking in another baby. Managing, without complaint or reflection, was a core standard of my mother's life.

My father's childhood stories were like precious pearls to me because they were so rare.

He seldom talked about his early life. He was the youngest of five and also grew up in poverty, but he never spoke, as my mother did, of longing for food or basic comforts. I was an adult when I learned that two of my father's older siblings had died before he was born. A brother died soon after birth and a sister died of poverty at age nine. She had a cold and the family had no food and no heat during the Wisconsin winter. I learned this story from my father's older sister. When I spoke to my father about the sister who died, Anna, he only acknowledged that it did happen. A brother who died at birth, the twin of his brother Bill, was never mentioned.

My father was a brilliant man, a wordsmith, a master storyteller and writer. He loved science and kept current with the latest scientific discoveries. He was adept at math, a scholar of political science, and a voracious reader of literature. He loved learning, although he wasn't able to attend college full-time until he was fifty-five. As a young man, he hungered for a college education. He told a story about asking his siblings for financial help to attend Clark University in Worcester, Massachusetts when he graduated from high school. Clark was offering him a scholarship but he needed an additional one hundred dollars. When his siblings didn't come through, he became a machinist and remained a factory worker for most of his working life. When I recounted this story to his sister, she told me that she had no recollection of being asked to help him financially. "Of course I would have helped him, my brilliant little brother."

A generous bequest by a neighbor made it possible for my father to quit his factory job at age fifty-five and become a full-time student.

He completed his bachelor's degree, and then a master's, in vocational counseling. A few years after he began working as a vocational counselor, helping men move from hospitalization for mental health issues to the paid workforce, he started to show signs of neurological impairment. He had a hard time focusing on more than one thing at a time. He didn't register pain, like the time he was hanging a picture and didn't notice that he was hitting his finger with the hammer rather than hitting the nail. I was alarmed by the injury to his finger, but not surprised that he didn't acknowledge the pain. It was a lesson I had learned all too well.

He would forget words, sometimes mid-sentence. The disease was never diagnosed. I thought it came from all the aluminum he inhaled as a machinist in an aluminum-can factory. The disease attacked his muscles, over time disabling his entire muscular system.

As the disease became more noticeable and interfered with his daily life, he didn't complain or ask for help, but he did begin to work at keeping himself as limber as possible. He endured. He stretched every morning for twenty minutes. He made homemade bread, which his grandchildren called "Zeda's good bread." Kneading the bread helped keep his hands supple. He went swimming twice a week at a pool in downtown San Francisco. The trip each way took about an hour. He took the No. 30 Express to the center of San Francisco and back, and then transferred to the No. 56, a local bus that only traveled through our neighborhood called Visitation Valley.

He knew the schedules and precisely where each bus was to stop. One day the No.56 pulled up about fifteen feet ahead of where it was supposed to stop. Slowly, my father made his way toward the bus. As he reached the door, he put one hand on the side of the bus to steady himself. At that instant, the bus started to move and the momentum caused him to fall. The rear tires of the bus rolled over his arm. People who were standing nearby said that my father yelled so loudly that the bus driver heard him and stopped the bus. His arm was de-gloved; all of the skin came off. After six weeks in the hospital for surgeries and skin grafts, he was unable to walk on his own. His illness progressed very rapidly from that point.

Within a year of the accident, he was living in the Jewish Home for the Aged on Silver Avenue in San Francisco. While he was still able to talk, he remained stoic, never showing irritation or agitation about his situation and rarely asking for anything. He continued to exercise as much as possible and he read about bus safety. When he discovered that the accident was not simply the driver's error but a systemic failure on the part of the SF transportation system to mount a five-dollar magnifying attachment to the rearview mirror on the passenger side of the bus, he sued the City of San Francisco. He outwardly directed his outrage. Change the system. Don't blame the little guy. He sued and he won. All busses in San Francisco now have a small circular mirror attached to the long rectangular mirror on the passenger side.

I never heard my father curse his misfortune or lament his limitations. Even as his muscles shriveled and his life became more and more limited, his focus was always the bigger picture, rather than his own suffering. After the accident, he was never able to walk unaided. He died five years later.

It took me years following the assault to disengage from my father's way of dealing with personal adversity and forge my own path.

My mother was bold; my father stoic. Both grew up in poverty and saw its effects on their own lives and the lives of so many others. As young people, each became involved in the Young Communist Youth League. My mother says she went to her first Young Communist Youth League meeting because she heard there would be food and dancing. She loved to dance and was always hungry. I don't know how their paths crossed. Neither ever spoke about their meeting or courtship, or their decision to get married. The only story I heard repeated was that they got married by a justice of the peace and then went out for an ice-cream soda. My father's father insisted on another ceremony, a Jewish one conducted by a rabbi. My father complied, but I don't think he ever stopped resenting the imposition of what he saw as a superficial religiosity into his life. Whatever brought them into the Young Communist League, my parents' lives joined and in large measure revolved around left-wing politics.

I was born after World War II ended, at the beginning of the anti-Red mania. My brother Eli, four and a half years my senior, remembers more of our parents' financial hardships than I do. Jobs were scarce and we moved frequently, often living with family members. As my father became more involved with labor organizing, he was often fired because of his political activity.

Both my brother and I were told never to talk about what happened in the family to anyone outside the family. As a young child, I understood this to mean simply: never talk. I knew there was something different about our family, mostly from schoolyard taunts of "dirty Jew" or "Christ-killer." During these years of my life we lived in Worcester, Massachusetts, then a manufacturing city with a diverse ethnic population. I don't recall having Jewish playmates. I heard my family talk in hushed tones about dangers to Jews. I didn't understand the conversations but I listened and gleaned from their worried looks that the world beyond my family was dangerous to Jews, so I thought that there was something bad or wrong about being Jewish, something wrong about being me.

My parents didn't talk about their politics directly. I knew little about what they were involved in and nothing about what it meant. I do vividly recall FBI agents lingering near our house and sometimes coming to our door to ask my parents questions. My parents never let them into our house.

As a young child, the idea of communists or FBI agents would, perhaps, have been less consequential for me but for the trial of Ethel and Julius Rosenberg. News of them blanketed my world. What I knew was that Ethel and Julius were Jewish and communists. I knew that they were going to be executed and that executed meant killed. I knew that the Rosenbergs had two children, aged seven and eleven, the same ages as me and my brother. I worried that my parents would be killed too. I became more resolute in my determination to keep silent.

I heard other children talk about Jews as devils. Communists were even worse, or so said the children on the street. I knew my parents and family members were kind and fun and I couldn't understand why they would be seen as devils. In the first grade, the teacher asked me to stand up and talk about the Jewish High Holidays, Rosh Hashanah and Yom Kippur. I can still recall the panic I felt. First of all, I knew nothing about being Jewish in terms of religion. My parents were not religious and neither practiced nor spoke about Jewish holidays or traditions. They would keep me home from school on the High Holidays to make the political statement that there were Jewish children in the school. I certainly didn't know one holiday from the next or what a High Holiday meant. This teacher "outed" me as Jew. I was identified and asked to speak as a Jew. It was a traumatic experience for me. I was the focus of the whole class. I don't know what I said or did. All I could think of was that I shouldn't talk about the family in public and that I didn't want to be known as Jewish. I didn't speak again in any class until I was in high school, nor did I ever tell my parents about my experience in school.

I grew up with secrets and silence, boldness and stoicism. I was smart and quick-witted. I loved to read and I absorbed new knowledge easily. I adopted my family's practice of examining external social structures and giving limited attention to internal struggles. My mother voiced great respect for people who "managed," who dealt with their personal travails without complaint, without medication, and without psychological intervention. My father accepted his life's disappointments silently, but he railed against the injustice meted out to others nationally and globally.

* * *

When I stepped out of the medical transporter with my life dramatically altered, I was accompanied by these things: my familial conditioning not to ask for help or talk about what I needed, a lifetime of admonitions to deal with the hand that's dealt, a lifetime of loving books, a passion for social justice, and the inclination to be silent, to keep my internal self hidden from others.

I didn't know that forging a new life meant I had to rely on others for everything, from being toileted to being driven and much more. I didn't know that it would be years before I could read more than a few paragraphs and even longer before I could focus on reading a book. I didn't know that my notions of justice and victimization and resolution would be dramatically challenged and altered. I didn't know that invisibility, once an ally, would become my tormentor. And I would continue to learn that the distance between silence and voice is incalculable.

Seven: Home Again and Other Sorrows

I looked around. Nothing seemed familiar. Home was a place I lived *before*.

Our house was sparkling clean. A beautiful bouquet of flowers sat in the middle of the round oak kitchen table with a note resting on one side of the vase: *We love you JoAnne.* Delicious smells from the meal prepared by our dear friend Arlene wafted through the house. So much thought and care had gone into making my return welcoming and I tried my best to be gracious and grateful. Rather, the person who spoke was appreciative and agreed that it was so good to be home. *I* was someplace else. My mind flitted from the gray wall of the alley to the searing white of the ICU, to the hospital bed I called home. I didn't want to be anywhere in particular. I just wanted to sleep.

I perched on the sofa as my friends tried to ensure my comfort. They put pillows under my arms. "Do you need extra pillows?"

"Are you in pain? Are you warm enough?"

"What a long drive. Are you tired? Hungry? Thirsty? Want wine?"

"No wine, thanks, but I'd love some dinner. I haven't eaten all day."

Arlene prepared a plate of food for me. She was a wonderful cook and knew my favorite foods. She offered me roast chicken, her special rice, and broccoli with slivered almonds. Debby moved toward me to cut my food and feed me. I felt embarrassed and self-conscious of my broken, bandaged, helpless hands. Arlene interjected, "Can I do that?" She lovingly cut my food and fed me. It was all so strange. Being fed. Sitting in a room that was both intimately familiar and in which I felt out of place. "Debby, I need to go to the bathroom," I announced.

The food was delicious, and I made an effort to eat with some enthusiasm, for the time and love put into the meal and readying the house for our return. I soon tired. Sitting up took energy. Listening required focus. I craved the solitude and comfort of being in bed. I needed to close my eyes and drift to nowhere.

Arlene and Martha cleaned up as Debby helped me undress. She found some clothes that were easy to take on and off and could fit over my bandaged arms. She arranged the pillows in mounds for my arms and my head. Once in bed, my body relaxed into the embrace of the mattress.

* * *

The days that followed my return are raggedy in my mind: somnolence surrounded by frenzy. I was like the ball in a pinball machine. There was so much to deal with and attend to, but I was unable to take responsibility for handling the tasks and barely able to even follow all of the details that needed attention. "Who can we call to arrange sick leave at the college? How should we handle the banking through your account? What else was in your wallet that needs to be canceled or replaced? What about the plane tickets to the Bahamas?" The questions went on and on and it seemed like things just happened. I'd answer, or try to, until another question brought me to a different place—a doctor's appointment, a visitor, a medical crisis, or a therapy of one kind or another.

Soon after we got home, Debby bought a large white board where she wrote what was happening on each day: where I needed to go, who was delivering food, who was driving me to which appointment, who was visiting, and anything else that I needed to know. Every time I got out of bed, I checked the white board to find out what day of the week it was and what I needed to do or remember, or just to keep me rooted in present time.

* * *

Before leaving D.C., Debby had made an appointment with Dr. Marianna Marguglio, my primary-care physician. She was leaving for vacation on January 30 and I needed to see her before she left. Dr. Marguglio had been in daily contact with Debby immediately after the assault and she followed every step of my treatment. On Thursday, January 29, I saw her. She appraised my overall condition and checked the incisions on my head. She greeted me warmly, without any visible reaction to my appearance, looked at the incisions and remarked that I was healing nicely. Seeing her became part of my weekly routine.

On Friday, January 30, we saw the hand surgeon. Part of my determination to return to Amherst during a snowstorm had to do with my hands becoming "sticky." By the time Dr. Refermat entered the examining room, he had already looked at the X-rays, CT scans, MRIs, and other medical information on the CD we brought home from George Washington University Hospital.

"Dr. Jones, I am so honored to meet you," he said. "I'm David Refermat."

I was sitting in a wheelchair and had to look up to see his gentle face. "Hello, Dr. Refermat, would you mind sitting in front of me? I can't look up." I felt so small and awkward in the chair as he seemed to tower over me. His smile and use of the honorific "Doctor" while greeting me helped me to feel comfortable enough to ask him to sit.

"Of course, I'm so sorry. I've already looked at your X-rays and medical reports. There is no need to take another X-ray. Your hands need to be operated on immediately. I usually don't like to do both hands at the same time but we really can't wait. It will be day surgery. You'll be able to go home in the early evening." His voice was soft and reassuring. "I know that this has been such a difficult and traumatic time for you. I'll do whatever I can to help you. What happened to you was so terrible." He gave Debby a business card and wrote his home phone number on it. "Call me anytime."

He was thoughtful, not patronizing or obsequious. He made me feel like a person with an injury rather than a seriously injured person. His compassion helped to ease the next medical ordeal.

Joan, a close friend, visited me within days of my return.

"Joan," I said as she was in the bedroom cutting the ends off of shirts so that they would fit over my casts. "Can you do another favor for me? Try to get the airlines to refund the money for the trip to the Bahamas I can't take?"

I had planned a grand month-long trip, the first I'd ever taken by myself. It was to happen after the inauguration. I had a lovely apartment rented on the island of Eleuthera, a rental car that would be waiting at the airport, my sabbatical material to work on, and the February sun and sand to enjoy. For a moment I recalled how enthusiastic I was while planning this trip, but even holding a good memory felt exhausting. I shifted my attention to the task that needed to be accomplished.

Joan dealt with the details. Bahamian Air offered a full refund once they received a copy of the police report. Another airline offered nothing and their response felt like a dismissal of the assault; it didn't rise to the standard of requiring action on their part. I wanted them to gasp at the brutality of what happened and respond quickly with a refund and wishes for a speedy recovery. I'm still disappointed.

✶ ✶ ✶

Bills mounted quickly. I didn't really know what they were for but I knew from the fast pace of Debby's questions that she was worried. "How much is the co-pay from Rachel Jenkins? You see her about twice a week. When is the mortgage payment due? We haven't received a bill yet from GW hospital. I'm not sure the insurance will cover everything. It's going to be huge. Did you know that the co-pays for your meds have gone up? It's fifty dollars for every refill. Do you think any of my costs related to the assault will be covered?"

"How do we get money back from the Compensation Fund for Victims of Violent Crimes?" Debby asked me. "Remember the woman who came to the hospital and talked to us about getting refunds for various medical services? You always called her the person with a kind face."

"All I remember is that she gave you a business card and some papers," I responded.

She found the business card from woman we called Kind Face, and we began a three-year interaction with the Compensation Fund for Victims of Violent Crimes. With the first call, Debby learned that Mr. Lee was to be our contact person. We would send the receipts for services related to the assault. He then checked each item, and in a month or so a check arrived for the amount that he approved. It was a business arrangement. I wondered: is violence from a gun worth more than from a hammer? Is a head injury worth more than a broken hip? What about paralysis? What about severe, incapacitating brain damage? How much is that worth in compensation?

At some point, he began to raise more questions about expenses related to the sequelae from the assault. He wrote, "I have some concern about a co-payment to Dr. Burbrick [twenty dollars] and co-payments for Clonazepam and Vimpat. It appears that the visit to Dr. Bubrick and the two mentioned medications are for treatment of seizures/epilepsy, which is a medical condition unrelated to any specific crime."

(letter dated November 13, 2012)

I wanted to write a long rant but only responded, "Both Clonazepam and Vimpat are anti-consultants to deal with the seizure I suffered as a result being beaten with a hammer in Washington, D.C."

Eventually we found out that the fund had a reimbursement limit. On a reimbursement form he simply noted, "You've reached your limit."

✳ ✳ ✳

Along with everything else Debby needed to do, she started a Caring Bridge website soon after we came home. It began as a means to get information and updates to family and friends. It soon proved to be a way for her to reflect and have a creative outlet. She became immersed in the telling of the story, and in doing so she could get detached enough from the grind of all that was required of her and have time with her own thoughts and feelings. At the end of most days, Debby got into bed, laptop propped on her legs, and told our Caring Bridge community about the events of that day. Her entries contained a litany of doctor's appointments, detailed descriptions of the food delivered to us every few days, delightful anecdotes about our many visitors, and typically a comment or two about whatever was current in the news that day. For almost two years, she wrote frequent entries on our Caring Bridge site, amassing hundreds of pages of entries and responses that would chronicle our daily events, struggles, and quirks. What she didn't write about was how the detritus from the assault sucked up the energy of our lives, demanding more and more.

Eight: Hand Surgery

Caring Bridge: Monday, February 2, 2009
Good Morning, Today is the day that Joanie is getting surgery on her hands. She slept well last night after a long day of organizing the Caring Bridge site and the very efficient schedule for Joanie's care . . . We will be going to Bay State Hospital in Springfield around 12:45 today in order to begin surgery at 2:15. We are very confident in the surgeon and the surgery is to last about two hours . . .

This surgery would join an endless string of medical episodes since I turned left into the alley behind Rachel's house. I knew the routine. Make a fist for a blood draw. Small pinch when the IV port is inserted. Johnnie ties in the back. Wear warm socks with raised grips on the bottom to protect against falling. Take off all jewelry. Lift your arms, move your legs. *What day is it? What is your birthday? Are you comfortable, Mrs. Jones?*

Yes. Thank you. I'm fine.

Bay State Hospital was a familiar and safe setting. Nurses hovered and spoke softly. They told me what to do and, with minimal elaboration, let me know what was to happen next. Nothing was required of me except to do what was asked. It is only in retrospect that I realize what was at stake with this surgery. What if something went wrong? What if my hands never functioned fully again? I didn't know the extent of injury on each hand and what was required to put the pieces of small bones back together again. I didn't ask questions. I didn't even consider what questions I should ask.

Debby and I waited together in the day-surgery prep room. We turned on the TV. Checked the clock. Changed TV stations. We didn't talk about the surgery. She was terrified and trying to be calm for me and I was fogged in, comforted by the familiarity of a hospital. "Do you want to watch the news?" I don't care. "Let's try *The Today Show*." Then a doctor I didn't know appeared, saying that he was my anesthesiologist, Dr. X. "I'm going to help you sleep, Mrs. Jones," he said in a jovial voice. "Don't worry. You'll be fine. When you wake up you'll see Dr. Y. He's taking over for me at . . . o'clock when I go off duty." I didn't catch his name, or the name of his replacement, or the time he mentioned, because it didn't matter. My job was only to bring my body to the operating room and then drift someplace. And he'd do whatever he did.

"OK," I responded.

Soon I was being wheeled into an operating room. I was still awake. The starkness of the OR surprised me. For a moment, I took in these new surroundings. I didn't recall ever seeing an operating room, because I'd been unconscious when I had brain surgery. Now, I was both curious and apprehensive. The room was so austere, so unwelcoming to my body. I was on a metal bed. The white walls and sheets and steel cupboards and instruments gave everything a grey tinge. "On my count." They really do say that. Someone counted to three and I was moved from the gurney to the operating table. Then Dr. X, the anesthesiologist, told me to count back from one hundred. For an instant I worried that I would get all the way to one and still be awake. "One hundred, ninety-nine, ninety-eight . . . "

I later learned that the planned two-hour surgery became a four-hour surgery. There was a problem with my left hand, the one already sticky. Dr. Refermat had to rebuild the titanium structure that would keep the small bones of my dominant hand in place. Surgery on my right hand went smoothly.

At some point after the operation, I vaguely heard someone calling my name. "Joanie wake up. Joanie wake up," the voice implored. I felt so far away from that voice and too tired to answer. I wanted to stay where I was. It was all white and very quiet. "I think I can sleep here for a long, long time," I thought, and saw my body curled in a corner. "I'm comfortable. I don't know if I can move. Just let me stay here a little longer. Please, let me stay here a little longer."

Now there were two voices. They got more plaintive. The sounds got louder and closer. I forced myself to open my eyes and saw Debby with our friend Bertha standing over me, calling my name. I felt so confused and tried harder to see them and hear them.

Later, I found out that I had a hard time coming out of the anesthetic. My breathing was labored and blood pressure low. Either Dr. X or Dr. Y or a nurse told Debby and Bertha to stand near me and call my name. They called for about forty-five minutes. When I heard their voices, I was just gaining consciousness and I was in pain. I missed the quiet, white place in my imagination that I'd had to leave.

It was some time, maybe a few years, before I grasped the intensity and danger of this post-surgical event. Debby was terrified as she saw me struggle to breathe and gain consciousness. She flashed back to the time when her mother didn't wake up and worried that I too would not awaken. At one point, she asked Bertha to stay in the recovery room with me so that she could go into the hall, crouch in a corner, and weep.

I heard a nurse say, "We'll have to admit her."

Yes. I'm safe. Back in a hospital.

My hospital room had two beds. The nursing staff settled me in one bed and Debby decided to spend the night in the other bed. When doctors made their morning rounds, they stopped first at Debby's bed to check on her medical status. She laughed, telling them that she was just visiting.

In the middle of the night, I woke up vomiting. I could barely move. My arms were ensconced in huge, pink Styrofoam holders—the kind used to pack fragile items for shipping—which made turning or moving almost impossible. Just the sight of them was overwhelming; they took up most of my field of vision, these massive, unyielding blocks of polystyrene, insulating me from my arms, reminding me of my complete helplessness.

My pain was intense and I felt nauseous. I vomited. I yelled out to Debby who called a nurse to help me. Even with the pain and disorientation that followed surgery, I was so embarrassed to be covered with vomit.

"I'm so sorry," I told the nurse.

"I see this all the time," she said, escorting me to the bathroom where she washed me and changed my clothes. She put on a clean johnnie and a pair of hospital-issue underpants that were at least four or five sizes too big for me. "I have to use the toilet," I whispered, tethered to an IV pole and overwhelmed by polystyrene. She helped me sit and then, to protect my privacy I presume, left me. In a few minutes, she knocked on the bathroom door, asked me if I was ready, and came in to clean me. With her help, I shuffled back to bed, complete with pink arms, wearing huge underpants and with a distinct *eau de vomit* aroma.

Dr. Refermat made his rounds before 6 a.m. I was comforted to see him. "The surgery went well," he said.

"When can these come off?" I asked, holding up my pink Styrofoam arms.

"I'm so sorry they are still on you. I only wanted them on for a short time. I'll give you a prescription for pain. Take them as soon as you get home. Try to stay ahead of the pain."

I was moved by his genuine concern for me, so I didn't tell him that I had no idea anymore when the pain started; it was just the state I lived in now—orbiting pain.

"I'll see you in ten days. Please feel free to call me anytime."

Shortly after he left, a nurse came in and removed the pink packaging, revealing swollen masses peering through casts that went from my knuckles to my elbows. My fingers were embedded in this protruding pink flesh. She told me to take the Styrofoam containers home with me and use them for pain relief.

The sight of these things hanging on my arms repulsed me. I felt hideous again, just as when I first saw myself in the mirror at GW hospital. I could feel despair settling into me.

A few hours later I was discharged, going home during another terrible snowstorm.

✷ ✷ ✷

Caring Bridge: Tuesday, February 3, 2009

Joanie is home! The hospital stays are over and she is onto recovery within her own home.

After hand surgery, I was in constant pain. Added to the exhaustion, headaches, and confusion was extreme pain in both hands. I started to measure time by when I could take the next oxycodone. My days were spent in bed, arms propped on pillows, moving in and out of a sleep state. Debby fed me and toileted me. If she had to be away, she asked a friend to be in the house in case I needed anything, to provide company, and to give me medication. I didn't want any visitors to take me to the bathroom, so her times away from the house were circumscribed by my needs and my never-ending worries.

Our relationship had always been one of mutual independence. We followed different work schedules, sometimes traveled at different times and had different rhythms for our leisure time. While we did many things together, I preferred quiet and solitude; Debby was more social and active. Now, I panicked when she would leave. I became more of an inquisitor: "Where are you going? When will you be home? Why do you need to do this or do that?" I was more petulant: "I don't want so-and-so to stay with me. I need you. What if I have to go to the bathroom?" She would answer patiently and try to meet my demands. She quickly squelched her own irritation, "OK. OK. OK. I know what YOU NEED. I'll be back, honey."

"How *are* you?" friends would ask Debby in plaintive voices, trying to offer her support and, I suspect, feeling relieved that they were not in our situation.

"I'm fine," she typically replied, murmuring the phrase from conventional marriage vows, "in sickness and in health."

My care required so much attention. She focused on me. She was a caretaker by profession and temperament, not inclined to see her own needs as priorities, and so the impact on her of the assault and my subsequent medical conditions went unspoken for several years. We began to talk much later, when I was stronger and she was more worn-out. "I wanted to take care of you and I felt it was my job to take care of you. I wouldn't let myself feel the weight of it. I was good natured for the first five years and then your hyper-vigilance about everything, always being tired, complaining about sounds and our lives, centered so much on the assault, began to puncture my denial. I wasn't fine. I was pissed . . . at you, at our situation, and at that fucker with the hammer."

＊ ＊ ＊

Caring Bridge: Wednesday, February 4, 2009
Unfortunately Monday (February 9) is the day that I will be returning to work and leaving my Joanie. This day has been difficult regarding the pain and she is eating just a little (especially when I forget to feed her). I wish that I'd forget to feed myself. She is still very interested in the news and thank god it's the Obama administration.

I still couldn't be alone. She began to contact home-healthcare agencies. We needed to hire a home-health aide to be with me during the day to feed, bathe, and toilet me. Debby found out the background of the aides and the range of services each agency provided. After many phone calls, we decided on the agency we'd use and established the date and time for my aide to begin.

There was still so much involving my care that needed attention. We needed food and I needed to be fed; I couldn't dress myself, or walk without support, or take medication without help, or wash my face, brush my hair, read without assistance, or even turn on the TV with my swollen, bandaged hands. While we—mostly Debby—got ready for in-home services, our friends Linda, Andy, and Margaret decided to develop a plan to support some of our other needs. They met together, and once the plan jelled, they came over to discuss the strategies with us. We all met in our living room. I was installed on the big green chair, arms propped on pillows and doing my best to follow the conversation. While much of the talk and most of the planning was about helping me, I was emotionally absent most of the time. Medication and brain trauma kept me tired. Confusion and the shock from trauma left me unable to focus closely.

They divided the tasks to be handled into three areas: food, transportation, and visits. Linda oversaw transportation, Andy tackled food, and Margaret, a way to manage visits. We said, OK.

The transportation calendar filled within an hour of being posted online.

We were soon deluged with food.

Visits happened at an orderly pace.

* * *

While grateful for the outpouring of support, I also felt awkward about having so many people coming in and out of our house. I often felt that I needed to make conversation or laugh at a joke or greet people personally when they dropped food off at the door. I, who had never wanted to ask for anything, now needed to ask for everything. This continuous helplessness added another layer to the growing Möbius strip of my life, with no discernable endpoint.

✳ ✳ ✳

Visits from the Visiting Nurses Association (VNA) began the day after I got home from hand surgery. In my traumatized mind, VNA nurses and therapists simply appeared in my bedroom. I'd open my eyes and there was a nurse checking my blood pressure, temperature, and pulse. Inspecting head incisions and reviewing medications. "Are you in pain?" "On a scale of one to ten, how bad is the pain?" "The incision looks good." "Someone will be back to check on you in a few days."

An occupational therapist from the VNA appeared. "Can you grasp a spoon? Reach for the phone? Hold a glass of water?" She talked about what she could arrange to increase the use of my completely swollen, plaster-encased hands.

A VNA physical therapist appeared. "Let's go into the kitchen; it's a great place to practice regaining your balance. Can you hold onto the kitchen counter and walk to the end of the counter? Then walk in the opposite direction. Stand on one leg holding onto the counter. Now the other leg." I tried to be good-natured, even though I just wanted her to stop talking and leave me alone. I didn't really care about my balance or walking to the end of the kitchen counter. I felt ashamed, like a child doing the most minor thing and being overly praised.

VNA overlapped with the health care aides until the end of February.

We contracted eight hours a day of health-care support, beginning the day Debby returned to work. For the first week or so, different women came either for a full day or for a four-hour period. Each was very pleasant, though for me their presence required a constant search for that Zen place as they brushed my teeth, took off my clothes to bathe me, and took me to the toilet, remaining in the bathroom to make sure I didn't fall, and then wiped me. I can no long remember the name of each person who came into our home, although two women remain clearly in my mind: Sonia and Janet.

Sonia came into the house calling out in a cheerful voice, "Hello sweetheart." "Do you want anything to eat darling?" followed by, "Do you want a bath, honey?" She was always jovial. But I was not her *honey* or *darling* or *sweetheart*, and these terms of endearment from someone who was there to bathe and toilet me only increased my sense of isolation and despair. She didn't talk to me when she wasn't performing a chore. With her, I felt like a patient and a body, and I found it difficult to muster either patience or gratitude. I felt awkward, naked, when she bathed me. Once I asked her to stay an extra hour because Debby was coming home late and I didn't feel safe being alone. "I'm only required to be here for four hours, Miss. I can talk to my supervisor and ask about getting more hours. I need to leave now."

Debby called the agency the next day. "We only want Janet as our health aide."

"Good morning," Janet called out when she arrived each morning. Still taking off her coat, she walked into my bedroom. "How are you today?" Before I could respond, Janet continued, "I'll get the coffee started and today I want you to eat more than a scrawny piece of toast. Did you always eat like a bird?"

She was more like someone I'd invited into my home, rather than someone doing a not- very-pleasant job. She talked to me about her children, ex-husband, travels, and professional ambitions. She talked to me like a peer while taking care of me. Because of this, I felt less self-conscious as she bathed me or dressed me. Sometimes she told me what was in the news or talked about anecdotes from her life and asked me questions about myself. "You have to get out of this house," she proclaimed in late March. "The Smith Flower Show just started and we're going to see it. I'll find some clean clothes for you to wear."

Janet continued to care for me until I was able to bathe myself, brush my teeth, and walk into the kitchen on my own. I was of course relieved to be able to care for myself, but sad to say goodbye to my friend Janet.

Visitors followed the time schedule that Margaret arranged, but talking to them required a huge amount of effort. I understand now that it's hard to know what to say to someone, particularly someone you care about, who has been bludgeoned with a hammer, whose cropped hair begins two inches behind her indented forehead, whose arms are in casts, who seems to have lost her signature sense of humor, her love of politics, and her passion for reading. The atmosphere around me was despondent, as is common for traumatized people. My visitors' well-meaning attempts to avoid asking about the assault made conversation even more difficult: "How are you feeling?" people commonly asked.

"Are you able to go to the movies?"

"How do your hands feel?"

"So, let me tell you about my day, my job, my child, my new car, my trip, my cousin's brain injury . . ."

"What do you think about how President Obama is doing so far?"

"What are you reading?"

"I'm not reading anything," I offered with no elaboration.

"Don't you miss reading? I can't imagine going through a day and not reading something."

I barely even understood the question. Reading was from *before*. Before, when I could stay awake, when my mind could focus, when my eyes could focus, when I could get outside of myself and think about a plot or news story and get lost in a mystery.

Other friends came over and sat silently or rubbed my feet. Some visitors read the newspaper to me. I enjoyed being read to, as long as the reader didn't mind when I closed my eyes and didn't want to talk about the news.

Savian, my then-eight-year-old grandson, often came into my bedroom. He sat on a chair next to my bed pretending to be concentrating on his Game Boy. Occasionally he'd lift his eyes toward me and I'd ask him to give me a sip of water. Then he'd gently lift a glass and straw to my lips. One day he brought me a get-well card from his school. He had made the card with some help from his teacher and asked all of his fourth-grade classmates and the teachers in the school to sign it. This card still hangs on the door to my bedroom. I was then, and I continue to be, so moved that he made such an effort to give me something that might make me happy. Now I also see this card as Savi's way to include his community in knowing about and connecting to this terrible event that shook his life.

I lived in a space of approximately one hundred square feet—the distance from my bed to the bathroom and to the green chair in the living room. My major activity was walking from the bedroom to the living room to sit in the big chair upholstered in green chenille, with rounded arms, cushioned back pillow, and a matching ottoman. The chair sits in front of a south-facing window, offering an eastern view to an open field and the Pelham Hills in the distance. I couldn't take in the world outside of the windows, but the shift from my bed-world to sitting with people at least brought me into something beyond my own thoughts. My thoughts swirled chaotically: I jumped from worrying whether Debby would remember to bring milk home to thinking about when I could take my next Oxycontin and perseverating about how to find a way to arrange my body so that both my hands and head were comfortable. Once I stopped fidgeting, images of the alley would suddenly appear, gray walls, sky and ground. And then fear, cold fear. I didn't know how to calm my mind. I just lay in bed and after a while—I don't know how long—I'd reach for the remote, find a crime show, and turn up the volume to block the thought-sounds in my head.

An excursion to the green chair typically meant someone was visiting.

"Your friend Gloria is here," Janet declared. "Let me comb your hair and get a clean shirt on you. Come on." She left no room for me to decline to leave the bedroom.

I liked Janet's direct manner. I didn't have to find a Zen place when she bathed or toileted me. It was her job and she was very matter-of-fact about these tasks. I perseverated less about the fact that I was sixty-two and needed someone to take me to the bathroom. It just was how things were. As our relationship grew, I was able to talk about how vulnerable and disoriented I felt.

"I feel so lost," I told her. "I'm never relaxed. Nothing feels familiar. I don't even know what I'm afraid of, but I always feel afraid."

"You know, I feel like that too, worried and anxious. At least you have a degree and a career. Look at me. I'm fifty-two and still cleaning people's butts . . . Oh, I'm so sorry."

Nine: Therapies

In 2000, during a time of personal and professional chaos, I had started therapy with Dr. Rachel Jenkins. I had tried therapy at different points in my life but found each experience to be of limited value. Dr. Jenkins was different—bold and direct, funny and insightful. I was comfortable with her and challenged by her. Astoundingly, she was able to connect my feelings and personal history within the context of being the child of Jewish communist parents. She was the first person to understand this context and provided me with a new lens through which to view my life. As soon as she offered her analysis, I knew it was right: I had always viewed my own concerns and needs as insignificant in relation to the vision of world change I'd heard about at my childhood dinner table. And even if my parents didn't tell me directly that my worries as a child were trivial, I heard their conversations and saw their anxieties about the pain and suffering of others. "That bastard Sukarno is the reason the people of Indonesia are starving . . . Papa Doc and Baby Doc, the evil father-and-son rulers of Haiti. And the United States government supports the Duvaliers. It's so outrageous. The people of Haiti suffer terribly. Look at what Castro is doing for the people of Cuba. They have health care now, and education."

They didn't speak about their own concerns or mention feeling sad or angry about something taking place in our family; they didn't ask about how my brother or I felt about a friend or a teacher or, most particularly, ourselves.

Our family had limited financial resources and my parents didn't prize material goods, yet as a child I wanted desperately to fit in with my peer group. I wanted to be like them and have things like the new clothing styles, not used clothing from Abby's New and Used clothing on Clement Street. Abby's sold "gently worn" women's clothes, not the hip styles of the 1960s. Perhaps I would have been more at ease wearing clothes that had been worn by young people. But Abby's sold *women's* clothing. I was a teen, short and thin. Nothing fit me properly. I remember a floral, shirtwaist dress. The colors were pretty but the belt needed to have an extra hole punched to fit my waist and the hem needed to be shortened three inches. It looked like my mother's dress that was altered for me. But I'd learned that I shouldn't complain, or talk openly about what I wanted, especially since my parents provided for all of my basic needs.

For my sixth-grade graduation from Visitation Valley Elementary School in San Francisco, I desperately wanted a pair of new, white, patent-leather flats, the kind without straps. All the girls had flats, but I wore brown and white oxfords. My father couldn't understand why I needed another pair of shoes since I already had a "perfectly good pair of shoes." My mother understood and took me shopping. She bought me a pair of white moccasins. I didn't want them. "They look fine," she asserted. "They don't even look like moccasins." I hated them, but what could I say? Who was I anyway to want new shoes, when so much of the world was suffering from not enough food? The terrible racism and poverty suffered by Southern Blacks. The grinding poverty of Appalachia. I didn't reveal my humiliation to my mother. I wore the shoes, hiding my deep disappointment, and pretended to not care when some of the kids made fun of my moccasins.

As an adult, I often dismissed my own concerns, wondering how I could I be upset about changes at work when I had a great job with benefits. And how could I be disturbed about my personal circumstances when I had so much? Yet I *was* disturbed and upset. The college had just eliminated the position I had held for several years. I still had a job but felt betrayed by the suddenness and scope of the change. At home, my stepson, his girlfriend, and their new baby were living with us. Neither had a job and we now had responsibility for a family of three. So despite my family's disdain for therapy, I sought guidance.

Dr. Jenkins helped me to understand how, in my child's mind, vast global concerns had always outplayed my worries. She showed me how I frequently felt caught between feelings of anger or resentment and my belief that others' troubles were much bigger than mine so I should simply acquiesce—wear the shoes I had and be grateful for them. She helped to deepen my grasp of how deeply wounded I was by the fears and hostility that permeated my life during the years of the Red Scare. She understood me and I trusted her.

After the assault, Debby had called Dr. Jenkins to let her know about my condition and provide some of the details of the assault. She had already seen the news in our local paper and was horrified and dismayed.

When she began to visit me at home, she sat in a chair right next to my bed. I don't recall our conversations but vividly remember how comforted I felt in her presence, the cadence of her voice and the sight of her curly hair and lanky body filling the space next to me.

A few weeks after the hand surgery, we started meeting in the living room, me curled on the green chair, her sitting on the white, slip-covered sofa. I tried to act like a host: "Can I get you some coffee? Some water?" I was putting on my "I'm OK" persona, even though she would have had to pour her own coffee.

She was the first person who I really talked to about the actual assault. I remember sitting on the green chair with my feet propped on the matching green ottoman. "Let's talk a little bit about that night. Just a little. Can you describe what happened when you got off the metro?"

I remember feeling some relief from her question. I was finally going to say, out loud, the scenes that played and replayed in my head. I began without hesitation, like an actor reciting memorized, well-rehearsed lines.

"I had been down the streets near Rachel's house so many times. I thought I was well prepared for the cold, but the wind was so biting. I turned down Tenth Street and just before the alley I passed a house that belonged to Rachel's friend. It was a beautiful house and I looked in the window, thinking I might see her. Then I turned into the alley and I felt something hit my head; I thought it might be a pebble dropping from the roof of a house."

"OK. Let's stop there," she said, bringing me suddenly back into my living room and away from the alley. "I think that's enough for now. Tell me how it feels to talk about what happened to you."

"I feel some relief. Some respite from going over and over the scene in my head. Now you have some of the story. Not just me. And I'm so very tired."

Small step by small step, Dr. Jenkins walked with me as I recounted my memories, put words to my horror and despair, and began the very slow climb from being hunkered down, deep inside of myself, to being able to move beyond the confines of my fears, fatigue, and trauma. As I clawed and thrashed my way through the aftermath of the assault, she helped me understand my resistance to expressing anger, even in the face of the heinous attack. It would be years, though, before I could dig into my emotional injuries: the magnitude of my fear, the anger that roiled inside of me, and my nascent but developing antipathy toward being diminished by anyone.

✶ ✶ ✶

In late February, a few weeks after hand surgery, I started occupational therapy at a center specializing in the rehabilitation of hands and arms. Debby took me to the first visit, which happened immediately after Dr. Refermat removed the casts. My hands looked like boxing mitts. They were pink, like meat ordered bleu red, and so swollen, like a toy that's been over-pumped with air. Had they not been part of my body, I wouldn't have recognized them as hands. I gasped and choked back tears.

"Don't worry. It's always a shock to see your hands soon after surgery. We'll have the swelling down in no time. Now let's get you fitted with removable casts. Just take them off to shower and then put them back on."

The very seasoned therapist saw my distress and immediately let me know that it was normal. She then proceeded with the next step. This was the start of a long and important relationship with hand-therapy specialists.

Julie was my OT therapist and over time we developed a strong bond. I talked about my work and family. She talked about her young son and extended family. She came to know me through our conversations and through my hands. There was an intimacy that passed between us that extended beyond the physical manipulations she did to my hands. She felt my pain, vulnerability, and fear though my hands. At first, she focused on reducing the swelling by the use of ultrasound. As my hands became less puffy, I moved to strengthening exercises and then trying to get greater mobility in my fingers. First I used the green clay, the most pliant. I squeezed and squeezed and squeezed, making different formations each time. Then I moved to the red clay, tougher to squeeze. Lifting light weights, picking up small objects from a dish with rice on the bottom, and putting objects on a ring—this was my weekly fare. At home I practiced many of the same exercises, sitting in the green chair with the clay and weights within my reach. Often the maneuvers were painful. Julie could tell when something caused me pain by the look on my face, though I never asked her to stop; I pushed through the pain. Over time the swelling went down and I could finally touch my thumb to my pinkie finger!

"I just touched my pinkie finger with my thumb, Julie! I did it! My thumb is moving. I'm so excited. It only took a month."

I spent so much time at OT, I felt like one of the staff. When interns began their rotation, they were often directed to work with me because I was able to tell them about the painful spots and the particular tools that tended to be most effective for this motion or that motion. I could also tell them what progress to look for: I told them that a big sign of change was when a patient began to wear jeans, rather than pants with an elastic waist. Jeans indicated the ability to fit a button into a buttonhole. I could instruct them on the rituals I now knew so well (sit for ten minutes under ten towels, gradual to intense exercise, homework until the next session).

Julie, the other OT staff, and the familiarity of the physical space became important beyond the recovery of the use of my hands. This was another caring community that saw me through the worst of times. I see it now as a place where I could heal my physical injuries and not only be "that person in the news who was beaten with a hammer," a phrase I'd heard the receptionist say to one of the clinicians. Most people at the clinic were there because of an accident of one kind or another. I wanted people to know that I did not have an accident—that my injuries were the result of violence. I couldn't then, and can't now, allow the assault to be lessened by the word *accident*.

Physical therapy began in late spring of 2009 in yet another location.

"Hi Mrs. Jones. So nice to meet you. Let's start. Can you tell me about your accident?"

"I DID NOT have an accident."

"Oh. Say, how did you get these injuries?"

I hated the retelling. I hated the cheery PT. I wanted to say, "I don't even want to be here. Don't want to talk to you or stand on one leg, or balance on a BOSU. I'll live with the dizziness and headaches . . ." Instead, I told an abbreviated version of my story. Usually, the hammer stopped all conversation.

Despite my positive experience with OT, I was tiring of specialists and exercises. Each one required retelling the story of what had happened to me. Each one required negotiating a new relationship, planning my time around the scheduled appointment and getting help with transportation. Each one required me to be a patient, an injured person, and a victim.

Now I understand that the therapies kept me attached to my traumatized status. While indeed there were significant physical and emotional hurdles to address, the trauma itself was becoming a cloak—something I could wrap myself up in, to maintain distance from ordinary life. I cleaved to my identity as the assault victim, ensconced by PTSD, with trenches of scars on my scalp to prove it. It gave me some cache. I was special, unique. Concealing my feelings came easily to me; speaking openly about the many impacts of the assault continues to be part of my healing process.

In June of 2009, I decided to stop physical therapy and go back to the gym. Before the assault, I'd been a gym rat. I had started running in my forties because all it required was a pair of shoes and could be done anywhere and by myself. To my great surprise, I both loved it and was good at it. I could run fast and for a long time. I liked feeling physically able. Running led to the occasional aerobics class and then becoming a full-fledged member of a gym.

I loved the gym. I took weight-lifting classes and aerobics classes. I took yoga classes, and when I wasn't in class, I used the treadmill. I usually worked out or took classes at 7:00 a.m. I would exercise, shower, and go to work feeling refreshed. A group of eight to ten women typically attended the 7:00 a.m. classes four days a week. Over time, we got to know each other and a sense of community developed. On those mornings when 7 a.m. came too early, I would pull myself out of bed knowing that my gym friends were expecting me. I felt fit and strong and energized—a major achievement for the girl in the blue one-piece gym suit who always got picked last for the team.

"I want to go back to the gym," I told Debby one day, sounding like a TV broadcaster announcing breaking news.

"When?" she asked, an ever-so-slight hint of fatigue in her voice.

"Tomorrow."

"OK. I'm free from 10–11:30."

✷ ✷ ✷

When we arrived at Gold's Gym the next day, the receptionist looked at me in surprise, and then asked, "How are you?" in a tremulous voice.

"I'm OK," I said and walked quickly toward the dressing room.

Debby followed me slowly, answering questions and providing details and stories of the assault and the days following. When I saw her head shake, I knew that the question was, "Did they catch him?" She handled the role of my spokesperson with aplomb. It suited her outgoing personality and her desire to protect me. But it also kept the emphasis of her life on my care.

Years passed before we talked how much of her energy was spent as my primary caretaker. About five years after the assault, we were having a small dinner party in our home. I did the cleaning, the menu-planning, and the cooking. When Debby came home only shortly before the guests arrived, I yelled, "You haven't done anything to help. I had to do everything!"

"Really! You're talking about a dinner?! Do you have any idea how many hours I have spent taking care of you, worrying about you, taking you to appointments?"

We both cried then, the pent-up emotions from those first years of our siege breaking through in an ordinary moment.

After a few escorted visits, I started going to the gym on my own. I was determined to get stronger. There was so much to practice . . . using my hands, strengthening my legs, developing better balance, focusing my eyes in different directions. At first, I stayed on the machines for a few minutes. Practicing. Practicing. Walking forward. Walking backward. Moving my legs. Gripping the machine to use my hands. Lifting free weights. After three months, in August 2009, I returned to aerobics classes and then tried a yoga class. For yoga, I always arrived just as the class began, sat near the door and left immediately when class ended. I tried not to make eye contact with anyone and gave only quick responses to a common set of remarks:

"You look great." *Thank you.*

"Are you all recovered?" *No. It will take a long time.*

"Did they catch the guy?" *No.*

"Are you back at work?" *Not yet. I'll return in the fall.*

I answered quickly, with practiced lines and little affect. If I lingered too long, I might start to *feel* the enormity of the assault, physically and emotionally. I didn't want to. It wasn't part of my emotional repertoire to explore feelings of vulnerability or anger, and I was single-mindedly intent on regaining my physical stamina, hand strength, and body balance. I couldn't yet afford to *feel.*

✳ ✳ ✳

Nearly six months had passed since the assault, and I really believed that I was almost healed. The story I told myself was this: My injuries were similar to a broken arm in a cast. The arm needs time for bones to knit, then it will be sufficiently healed, maybe not like before the break, but strong and useful. I didn't believe that my bones had fully knit, so to speak, but enough for me to keeping plugging forward. My story continued: As I regained physical strength, I would be less tired.

Twice a week I saw Dr. Jenkins for psychotherapy. At the time, I didn't realize the extent to which I was still reeling emotionally.

"Are you going out of the house? Seeing friends or going for coffee?"

"No. Not yet. I'm still weepy all the time. Yesterday I bumped my head on the wall behind the bed and broke into tears. I cry so easily now. What if I'm with someone having lunch and I start to cry?"

"So, you cry. Then what happens?"

"I don't know. The truth is I don't care to be with . . . with anyone. I really don't."

"I've been thinking about your isolation. I think you have a psychological condition called *anhedonia*," she offered.

I learned the definition of anhedonia: "The loss of a sense of pleasure; for example, an ability to be thrilled by a glorious sunset or respond to music that formerly was passionately loved" (Osborn). I used to love going to movies, having dinner with friends, being in the sun, planting flowers, and especially spending quiet nights at home with Debby, giggling about nothing. In truth, I had no sense of loss. I didn't realize how removed I was from ordinary life.

The assault provided indisputable reasons to pass up going to a movie or taking a trip or going out to dinner or even talking on the phone. Debby gave my apologies to people. "Joanie's tired. Joanie has a headache. Joanie won't be able to be around so much noise, so many people, so much talking, so much stimulus . . ."

It is only in retrospect that I've realized how emotionally flat and unavailable I was for much of the first year following the assault. At the time, I didn't feel the loss of things that were once pleasurable. I didn't realize or even think about what it must have been like for Debby, or Rachel, or Savi, or friends to be around me now. I didn't feel at all.

Experiencing life-threating violence and sustaining serious injuries alters life as it once was and inevitably leads to heightened self-absorption. Caring Bridge eloquently captured my life for the first two years after the assault. It was a life that seemed to orbit inside its own tiny atmosphere. People came to see me—Rachel, my brother, sisters-in-law, nephew, and best friend—and the commentary was about their interactions with me. Friends came and talked, or rubbed my feet, or read to me.

February 10, 2009: Joanie had a good night where she slept six hours straight!!! We awoke and got Savi off to school and then the VNA nurse and a VNA home health aide arrived. Joanie will be having a health aide for about ten hours a day.

April 14, 2009: Just a short note to inform you that Rachel is here! Joanie is tired but beside herself that her little girl is here. They are planning to go to lunch tomorrow at the new burger and fries place in Northampton.

June 28, 2009: Wow, Eli left today after a four-day visit. Martha was here for only one day, but will be back in September. So, after Sheila left we have a Martha/Eli visit and then on Tuesday, Mary arrives.

March 9, 2009: Tomorrow is another day and each day is filled with luscious gifts and attention from our friends and family. The horror of Joanie's incident lies sometimes flat, sometimes floating behind us all as we help each other heal. We are all healing each other. This D.C. incident traumatized us all, vicariously and/or directly. Thank you for walking beside us and stepping up as we learn to manage our life as it is today.

Re-reading these Caring Bridge entries much later, I felt embarrassed that my attention toward others was so minimal. I can barely elicit even vague recollections of the important events in the lives of those who love me so well.

Now, when I meet someone who has recently experienced a tragedy or suffered a serious trauma, I recognize the plexiglass-like casing that once surrounded me. The person can be clearly seen but not accessed.

Physical and occupational therapy helped me to regain my strength, but it was Dr. Jenkins's strong and guiding support and skill that enabled me to gradually experience pleasure again.

Ten: Back to Work;
Down the Up Staircase

At the time of the assault, I was a full professor with tenure, seven years from retiring from a forty-year career of teaching in higher education. I earned a good salary with excellent benefits, though I worried about finances and sick leave, as if I was a factory worker like my father or a secretary like my mother.

By mid-July 2009, I had been on sick leave for almost eight months. I felt like I *had* to return to full-time work. I worried that my paid sick leave was almost used up. I worried about how I could manage financially if I didn't get a full paycheck. I didn't think there were any other options. I saw only two choices: be sick or work full-time. Work was what I did and what gave me a sense of identity. Besides, I believed that I was on the mend and could handle whatever challenges I might face, though I wasn't really clear about what those challenges might be.

I called the human resources department of the college.

"Hi. I'm planning to return to work August 1, 2009."

"Are you one hundred percent?"

Who is? I said to myself.

Debby shepherded me on the first brief visit back to my office. I managed to get through the initial round of *welcome back*s and *how are you*s and just sad looks. I opened my office door and tried to do some preliminary organization: open email, look at snail mail, check for phone messages. I soon tired and we left after an hour.

Just before returning to full-time status, I found new reading materials for my classes, reorganized my course syllabi, and ordered textbooks. I spent time thinking about new ways to present and engage students in the course content. The courses weren't new to me, and *before*, I'd had ample energy for the eight-hour teaching days. I had always relished the teaching schedule that was designed to offer an intense classroom experience in one day rather than a few hours several evenings a week. Now I worried about getting through the day and began to get apprehensive about returning to the classroom.

My first class was scheduled to begin on September 12, 2009.

I woke up in the middle of the night on September 8, lying in my own excrement. It was the consistency of diarrhea, though I had had no discomfort. I was so ashamed. "Debby, get up. Just get up. I'm lying in diarrhea but I'll clean it up right now." I changed the sheets and we both went back to sleep.

During the day, I ruminated about what had happened but since I felt fine, I decided it didn't mean anything other than perhaps the agonies of aging or the anxiety about returning to work.

I took Savi to his soccer game in the late afternoon on September 8 As the warm fall day turned to evening, I became aware of a chill in the air and then felt a sharp pain in the back of my head. I had always been bothered by cold, and cold wind in particular, so I assumed this pain was connected to simply being cold. The game ended and we headed home. The throbbing did not subside. By the time I got home I knew I couldn't take care of Savi. I called Debby and told her that she needed to get home as soon as possible. When she arrived, I went to bed.

About 4:00 a.m. on September 9, I woke up with severe abdominal pain. It was unlike anything I had ever experienced. Sharp. Intense. Agonizing. I got out of bed and went into the bathroom so as not to awaken Debby or Savi, who by then had crawled into our bed. The last thing I recall, I was sitting on the toilet seat . . .

✳ ✳ ✳

"Joanie, wake up. I called 911. Joanie, wake up." It was Debby's voice but I didn't know what she was talking about. I heard her say, "I just called 911. Wake up. Wake up."

"I don't have any pants on. I need to have pants on," I muttered. Soon, two young men pushing a gurney were standing at our bathroom door. Debby told them that she heard me make a sound after I got out of bed, and when she came into the bathroom she found me sitting on the toilet, my head slumped down. The angle of the face that she could see was contorted and one arm was twisted forward. She ran for the phone in our bedroom, closed the door so that Savian wouldn't hear, and tried to prevent me from falling as she called 911. When the EMTs arrived, she told them about the assault and the medication I was taking. I was conscious when the ambulance arrived.

"What's your name?" one of the young men asked. "JoAnne," I mumbled. "Don't worry, JoAnne, we'll take good care of you." They wheeled me to the ambulance and Debby said she would follow as soon as possible.

Another ambulance. This time, I heard the siren. The EMTs were taking my blood pressure and pulse and calling the information in to the ER doctors at Cooley Dickinson hospital. Familiar questions: "What's your name? What is today's date? What year is it? What is your birthday? How do you feel? Can you raise your leg? Can you follow my finger with your eyes?"

I don't remember much of the ride or arriving in the emergency room. After some prodding and questions, I was told that I would have to be admitted immediately for more extensive testing. I was no longer in any pain but I was very, very tired.

When Debby arrived, she had the CDs from GW Hospital

showing the treatment I'd received in Washington. She gave these to the on-call doctor who then prescribed a CT scan, an EEG, blood tests, and X-rays. I slipped easily into the role of patient. I cooperated. I didn't think about what had just happened in part because I wasn't conscious when it took place. It joined the other blurs circulating through me. I was in a hospital. I made a fist for blood draws, made sure not to jostle the IV port, and thanked everyone who came into my room to take my blood pressure or bring food. I wasn't afraid. Actually, being back in a hospital was comforting. I didn't have any pain and at that point didn't know what had happened to me.

I spent the night of September 9 in the hospital, mostly listening to the night sounds of carts moving in the hallways, patients calling for help, and the *bleep* of the machines monitoring my heart, oxygen levels, and blood pressure.

The hospitalist on duty, Dr. Q, came to see me in the early morning hours of September 10 to announce the next set of tests I had to undergo.

"OK." What else could I say?

I began to feel anxious as soon I was placed on a gurney. "Where are we going?" I asked the orderly.

"I'm just the driver, ma'am. Taking you to nuclear medicine. Don't worry, I'll be staying around until I drive you back to this room."

I could see my hands and I knew that with work they had gone from broken to swollen to functional. I didn't think about my brain. Now I did. "This fucking nightmare will never end," I mumbled. Now I was afraid.

✶ ✶ ✶

In mid-afternoon, Dr. Q returned to my room. "Yup. Almost certain you had a seizure. Given the severity of your head injuries, there's nothing else it can be. I've asked our neurologist to see you." He didn't share the results of any of the tests I had undergone. At that moment

I was alone in the room and there was no one to ask questions on my behalf. He spoke quickly and my thoughts moved slowly. A seizure sounded like a lifetime sentence of health problems and limitations. I didn't really know what to say and he didn't offer any additional information or words of assurance.

Soon after he left, a neurologist came in, introduced herself and confirmed the diagnosis. "No doubt," she proclaimed in a strong voice. "I'll start you immediately on anticonvulsant medication." The symptoms I described before coming to the hospital, pains and diarrhea, were auras, she offered, all foreshadowing a seizure. "I'm surprised this didn't happen sooner and surprised you didn't have a stroke. These typically happen with injuries like yours."

"Why did I have a seizure?" I asked.

"The scar tissue in your head impedes the smooth transmission of electrical impulses, causing a seizure or a stroke. It's a very common side effect of traumatic brain injury." She was matter-of-fact and added, "I'm moving away from this area. You'll need to find a neurologist to treat you. I'd like you to stay in the hospital over the weekend so we can see how you react to the anticonvulsant medication. I'll have to report the seizure to the RMV. You won't be allowed to drive for six months."

I was devastated. Driving was my access to independence. I was emotionally careening to a place of despair. I had been crawling my way back to life for eight months already. Six more months felt endless. I felt punished for thinking I was getting better; punished for being assaulted.

＊＊＊

Caring Bridge: September 9, 2009

We have some new difficult news. Joanie had a seizure, which the neurologist said is not unusual for people with the severity of her brain injury. Apparently the scar tissue that forms in the brain interferes with the electrical currents and makes them go somewhat haywire. (Medically speaking.) The Dr. put together the threads of information such as the sudden and short-lived abdominal pain, the scrunching up of her right hand, how she was seated and, of course, her brain injury. She said that people don't typically faint sitting down. We are still trying to absorb the information. We are learning how her fatigue, digestive problems and other things lowered her seizure threshold and contributed to this happening . . . We both will have to, ONCE AGAIN, ask for help.

Seizure. The word terrified me. What would my life be like now? Would I continue to have seizures? What did this all mean? I had just resumed driving a few months before. Classes were starting the next day. I had to be in class tomorrow. I had to start classes. I had to.

When the hospitalist came back to see me, I told him that I had to be discharged. I pleaded with him. In spite of his strong concerns he agreed to sign the discharge order and I promised to return to the hospital as an outpatient on Monday, September 14 for more tests. There were always more tests.

I was determined to be present for the first day of classes after my long absence. This resolve was not about meeting a work expectation or work commitment, although that was important to me. Its powerful energy came from someplace else, similar to the energy that compelled me to stay with Rachel in Washington and leave during a snowstorm. Maybe I still had some links to my grandparents, who fled the pogroms of Russia with no money and no ability to speak English, or to my parents who stood up to fascism of various kinds. Or maybe this was just my will to live.

I had to leave the hospital and meet my class the next day. The concept of a seizure and consequences I didn't know certainly lingered on the periphery of my thinking. But being present and visible for the first day of classes—showing up for the role I'd held for nearly forty years—crowded out all other considerations.

The seizure meant I was again unable to drive and needed transportation help. With a few phone calls, rides were arranged.

I was up and out of bed at 6:00 a.m. on September 12, much earlier than necessary. I felt anxious about everything: *Am I wearing the right clothes? How do I look? Are all of my materials ready? Will I have the stamina to last all day? How will I deal with all of the questions and comments from people who haven't seen me since classes ended in 2008, a lifetime ago?*

I had asked to be assigned a classroom in the same building as my office so that I didn't have to walk across the campus after dark. I needed to reduce the number of circumstances that might cause me to wonder about my safety and thus appear to be other than perfectly relaxed and in control. I needed to reduce the chances that I might remember and *feel*.

When I walked into my classroom on September 12, I put the juice and donuts that I'd bought for everyone to share on a table. Classes were scheduled for a full day, part of the condensed program structure that permitted students to work during the week and be in school only on weekends. Food makes any setting feel more comfortable and so I always brought food to each class. As students entered, I asked them to help me move some of the chairs and invited them to have some food.

"Good morning. I'm Dr. JoAnne Silver Jones . . ." I began.

My anxieties soon melted away as students greeted me with hugs and tears. "You've been in my prayers, Dr. Jones."

"I am so glad to see you, Dr. Jones."

"God brought you back to us, Dr. Jones."

I was blanketed with a kind of love and concern that had nothing to do with questions about the assault or the state of my health. I didn't have to be anything other than myself and present to be showered, unconditionally, by their grace.

Eleven: Trauma and the Adult Classroom

"What should we call you?" students had often asked me. "My name is JoAnne," I typically replied, thinking that the use of my first name, rather than academic title, put me on more equal terms with the students. It was my comfort, not theirs, that had shaped my behavior.

"OK, Dr. Jones," was their frequent response.

＊＊＊

I had taught in higher education for almost forty years. It wasn't a childhood ambition. My major ambition as a young woman was to marry and try to be a "normal" married woman with children, a turned-up nose, and pageboy haircut. I also wanted to be a pediatrician. As with so many young women, I struggled with seeing myself as different from the Donna Reed media image of my coming-of-age era. Donna Reed was not the representation of a Jewish woman. She didn't work or go to college. I didn't know women who were professionals, like professors or doctors or lawyers, but I did grow up in a family that prized education. My mother always worked, as did the mothers of all of my friends. I had never heard of a stay-at-home mom.

A few years after completing my undergraduate degree and one year of a master's program, I started teaching in an experimental undergraduate program in social work at the University of Calgary. The experiment was to engage students in dialogue rather than rely solely on lectures, and to use life experience as a significant foundation for learning. In that experiment I found my calling. I loved the classroom and this "new" mode of teaching came easily to me. After a few years, I decided to get a doctorate in a program that focused on education.

Most of my work had been with adult students, primarily women of color, who never thought they'd be in college. Many had become mothers at an early age and were now single parents, working two or three jobs to support their family. They prized learning and struggled to ensure that their children had the opportunity to go to college. Their own stories were of counselors who steered them toward technical schools and away from higher education. "Get a skill and then you'll always be able to support yourself. I'm just not sure you're college material." They were often first-generation college students with no family examples to follow into advanced education, nor people in their lives entitled to the honorific title of Doctor. Going to college frequently required great sacrifices.

Comments taken from student papers, 1998–2001:

"Well, I get up at 5:00 a.m. every day to study before I get my kids up at 6:30. I study again from about 10:00–midnight when my kids go to bed, unless I'm working a double shift and then I make sure dinner is ready for my kids and bring my books to work."

"My doctor said I should quit school while going through chemo. He doesn't understand. School is what is keeping me alive."

"My husband doesn't like the fact that I'm in school. He says I'm not being responsible for my family. So on school weekends, get up at 4:30 a.m. and make the coffee, finish the laundry and get the dinner all ready so it just needs to be heated when I get home. He still gets angry."

✳ ✳ ✳

Almost all of the students I've worked with, women and men, entered the college classroom with a mixture of fear and excitement, and usually questioning their intellectual abilities. I didn't fully understand that they insisted on calling me Dr. Silver Jones because my status legitimized *their* status as college students. We were not, in fact, equal in this setting: they needed me to be the professor.

I loved the adult classroom and had a deep vein of knowledge and understanding about the craft of teaching. My anxiety about returning to teaching on September 10 was born from traumatic brain injury, a seizure, and post-traumatic stress syndrome. Would my words flow? Would I remember the sequence I wanted to follow? Would I garble words or misspeak? I spent hours preparing the courses that I'd taught for years.

Traumatic brain injury sapped my strength and diminished my focus. The particular part of my brain that was injured was the frontal lobe. I, who was always so organized, able to engross myself in the process of writing or reading, able to find my way on roads or through complex problems, now got lost. I passed familiar roads and took wrong turns. I read less and less. The joy I once felt at finding new materials and connecting current issues to the themes of a course was replaced with being hyper-focused on reviewing and rehearsing the material I knew well, afraid ideas might fly out of my head. And perhaps the most difficult symptom to handle was the grinding fatigue that was my ever-present companion.

After I returned to work, I soon found ways to incorporate what I was learning about PTSD and TBI into my teaching; the more I understood my own PTSD, the more insight I had into the experiences of so many of my students. Traumatic reactions happen for a whole variety of reasons. While many adults had experienced particular traumas in their personal lives, I realized that the vast majority of the students I worked with were products of schools that did not prepare them for college. They missed the part of college preparation that instills confidence and the belief that one belongs in college and can successfully complete a degree. This preparation is not only about English grammar or algebraic equations. Lack of confidence, lack of preparation, and a history of limiting and often humiliating experiences are traumatizing products of systemic racism and classism.

I clearly saw and felt the signs of trauma in my classroom. After the assault, I realized that when some students asked the same question over and over again, it was not because they lacked interest in the course material, but because stress impaired their ability to absorb what was said. I saw their fear of speaking and writing in a new light. I saw how they repelled my attempts at positive feedback, like a raincoat repelling water. Trauma obstructed new self-awareness from filtering into their conscious minds. I could feel their visceral fear of the professor's authority; no matter how many times I used to say "call me for help," few ever called.

Before the assault, I knew that this fear was present, and I thought that by naming it and telling people, in so many words, that I was a nice, fair person who wouldn't hurt them, we could move on. After the assault, I had more patience. I now understood that feeling safe takes time. Now, my words of support were not only a means to get to the "real" stuff of learning. Knowing how to reduce fear, feel safe, and focus on the present *is* the learning. I understood that until students felt safe, their bodies and minds remained on guard.

Before, I used to rearrange the chairs before class so that students were sitting in a horseshoe configuration rather than straight rows with only limited eye contact between participants. When someone entered the room, I would invite that person to take a seat in the circle. I wanted to create a sense of community through the organization of chairs. While I used the language of invitation, I gave the message that sitting in the circle was *my* preference. Now, though my desire to create community didn't change, I was much more aware that community happens best when no one feels threatened or unsafe. I would still do some rearranging of the room. I myself was no longer comfortable sitting with my back to the door or feeling crowded by sitting in between people. Now, I invited students to choose wherever they wanted to sit and to feel free to change seats during the day.

Before, I used to provide many opportunities for students to comprehend the assignments and grading rubric. *Before,* I would spend the first hour of class carefully going over the syllabus and then move on. I was not able to completely disguise my annoyance when someone asked the same question over and over, or, in my assessment, didn't seem to be listening, thereby missing important details.

Now, I understood more about how trauma blocks both attention to and absorption of information. After the assault, I could hear the same information repeated many times, but fear was the loudest sound that reverberated in my head. I worried that I wouldn't be able to follow everything that was said and I'd be embarrassed. I knew the feeling of being flooded or overcome by too much information and stimulation. I needed time to take in what I heard. So now, I spent less time on all of the details of the syllabus and concentrated on what I thought were the few most important things to know in the beginning. I spent the same amount of time as before, but on less information and with no expectation that everything I said was being understood.

I also developed more ways to give mental breaks during a class. Sometimes I'd invite the class to play a silly game, or offer five minutes of quiet time, or play some music, or give some time for just talking, off-subject.

✳ ✳ ✳

I'd already had a major lesson about PTSD in 2001, when a student in one of my classes had approached me after class. Cheryl said, "I think John, my ex, would be a good speaker for this class." *Oh no,* I thought. *Just what I don't need, dealing with someone's ex. I teach, I don't get involved in the stuff of someone's life.*

"He's a Vietnam vet," she continued.

My sense of dread increased. The country was filled with patriotic fervor following the recent attack of September 11, 2001. I didn't know his politics. I believed in education as the marketplace of ideas, but in my class I wanted to guide those ideas.

"Sure," I responded, reluctant to discourage her enthusiasm.

I couldn't have imagined that John, or Big John as he preferred to be called, would become a regular part of my class and an important part of my life. His first day in my class was on December 20, 2001.

"Hello. I'm JoAnne." I held out my hand to a tall, large, light-skinned man wearing a baseball-style cap with a First Cav (for Cavalry) logo and a black motorcycle jacket also decorated with military patches.

"Nice to meet you, Dr. Jones."

John had never spoken before a group. I introduced him to the class and then, intuitively, I think, sat down behind him. He started talking—or rather, he started rambling. I quickly learned that he had been part of the First Cav, and that that designation had remained a central part of his identity. Prompted by Cheryl, he spoke of other parts of his life, including being bi-racial, born to a mother from France and a father from Louisiana.

"I hated my father. He was so hard on me. Life was all work. He never came to any of my football games. He expected me to be the example for my three younger brothers. I couldn't have friends over to our house. Every year Dad and his brother went to see their mom in Louisiana. I would listen as they mapped out their route, careful not to drive during the daylight in certain areas. I didn't know then that he was trying to protect us from the Jim Crow world." He stopped momentarily, swallowed and continued. "I learned about the South myself when I went to Louisiana to help take care of my grandmother. I was thirteen. I learned then what was meant by the 'other side of the tracks.' I realized why my father was so hard on me. His lessons saved my life in Vietnam because I knew how to deal with stress, how to think quickly, how to be scared and not buckle . . . He died before I could tell him how much I loved him . . .

"I'm pretty sure my younger brother left Vietnam on the same plane that brought me in, but he left in a body bag. He was only nineteen . . . wanted to prove himself to me, I think," John said, choking back tears. "He was younger, smaller and darker than me . . .

"When I got off the bus in Hartford, Connecticut, I was wearing my uniform. I'd been in Nam that morning and now I was in Connecticut. I saw an older woman. She spit at me and called me a baby killer. I hung up my uniform that night and have never looked at it again. No one ever welcomed me home."

When John finished speaking, Bill, a student from Nigeria, stood up and said, "Welcome home, John." All members of the class stood and gave John an ovation. John wept. We all wept.

For the next ten years, John came to my classes on the last day of the term. I always sat behind him, and he only talked about his war experience and his PTSD in my class. I began to see the interconnections of his PTSD experiences as the son of a black man whose life was forged in the Jim Crow South, as a veteran who had witnessed the racism and lies in Vietnam, and as a man who had lost his brother to the war. The Gordian knot of trauma was clearly displayed through his story.

* * *

Soon after I was assaulted—as soon as I could hold a phone—I called John. I knew he would understand. I knew from his story that trauma was an ever-present shadow companion. I knew that talking about trauma begins with words tumbling out, jumping across time, sometimes told without punctuation or elaboration, and sometimes offered with every detail. John taught me that the aftermath of trauma could be littered with bad decisions and lead to self-recriminations. He taught me about the importance of having someone at your back, and that it's OK to keep your own back to the wall. He taught me that one's personal history—social, emotional, cultural, and historical—is like a helix, a spiral, surrounding the trauma, and serves to both exacerbate and ameliorate healing.

As I trudged through my own healing process, I remembered how many years John had spent denying his PTSD, clinging to the image he'd forged as a child of the strong man who soldiers on, suppressing feelings—the decades consumed as he peeled through layers of family admonishments and the cultural and political impact of racism and the Vietnam War. Slowly, I was coming to see how healing meant probing through the tiers of my life and investigating the wider context in which each layer was situated.

So when I walked into the classroom on my first day back, I could feel the tremors of fear as students sat in an environment—school—that for many had been a fount of trauma. I tried my best to reduce their obstacles.

Twelve: Doctors Extraordinaire

With the addition of seizures to my life, I needed to have more medical and pharmacological intervention. I had to quickly find a neurologist. One more issue. One more roadblock. One more strategy.

A friend suggested Dr. Ellen Bubrick at Brigham and Women's Hospital in Boston. The distance from home became a secondary consideration to my desire to have the best medical care. I called for an appointment. Dr. Bubrick, like other doctors at BWH, saw patients only a few days a week and taught at Harvard Medical School the other days. Appointments with her were very difficult to get.

"I'd like to make an appointment with Dr. Bubrick. I had a seizure a few weeks ago."

"Dr. Bubrick is only taking new patients who have special concerns. Can you tell me about your recent medical history?"

"I had a craniotomy in January, the result of being beaten with a hammer," I said, trying to be matter-of-fact and feeling tremulous.

"Oh my. Let me check her calendar . . . She can see you in a few weeks."

* * *

The day of the appointment, Debby and I sat in the waiting room of the neurology department at Brigham and Women's Hospital. As usual, I was anxious. Waiting rooms all seemed to have a common quality: identical chairs upholstered in sturdy material in neutral tones. No space between chairs. Tables with magazines, often on medical subjects, or outdated magazines like *Women's Day* or *Time* lay piled in front of the chairs or in nearby racks. All eyes face forward as patients wait, in various forms of discomfort, for the moment when their name is called.

"JoAnne Jones?" A lovely young woman wearing a white doctor's coat and a broad, welcoming smile called my name.

When she saw me stand, she walked toward me, hand extended.

"Hi. I'm Ellen."

"So nice to meet you, Dr. Bubrick," I responded.

Prior to this appointment, she had already seen the MRIs, X-rays, EEGs, and CT scans from George Washington University Hospital and Cooley Dickenson Hospital.

"I'm so sorry that this horrible event happened to you," she offered immediately.

She asked Debby to describe the morning of the seizure. When Debby finished, Dr. Bubrick confirmed what we had heard from the neurologist at Cooley Dickenson, although in a softer voice and with her eyes meeting mine.

"There is no doubt that you had a seizure. More typically, someone with your injuries would experience a seizure or stroke closer in time to the injury."

She asked about our family and our work. She listened to our answers. She explained again what led to the seizure and assured me that she would now pay careful attention to my neurological health. Then she gave me her email address and cell phone number and invited me to contact her anytime I had questions or worries. She was kind, compassionate, and comforting.

During my second visit with her, I told her about my constant and extreme fatigue and other ongoing symptoms of trauma. "I am hyper-vigilant, startle often, and cry frequently, sometimes over a loud noise or just feeling a twig touch my head . . . I'm always very tired."

She responded quickly, "I was so shaken by what happened to you when we first met that I forgot to make a referral to Dr. El Chemali. You'll love her. We are good friends. She's a neuro-psychiatrist that specializes in trauma."

* * *

With Dr. Bubrick's support, I was accepted as Dr. El Chemali's patient. Her practice was also limited. As always, Debby went with me to the first appointment. Same hospital, same look to the waiting room, but with the chairs in a different configuration. Dr. El Chemali called my name and I looked up to see another beautiful young doctor. She didn't move at first and then signaled me to follow her. When we got to her office, she held out her hand, introduced herself and said, "I must tell you that I was taken aback when I saw you. I've looked at all the medical records and thought there must be a mistake when you stood up, walked, and looked so good, given the severity of your injuries. I'm amazed at how well you are doing." I felt proud hearing her words. She knew what had happened to me and she understood the trajectory of recovery from head trauma. She was stunned with my recovery.

She showed me, viscerally, what safety feels like. She held the weight of my trauma through her clarity, kindness, and competence. She gave me, and continues to give me, the space to see how the trauma lives in me.

She asked me questions and patiently listened to the answers. She wanted to know about my work and my family. Then she asked about how my life had changed since the assault: How did I feel? What was difficult for me? And what questions did I have?

I asked, "What might happen to me next? What actually happened in my brain? Will I get worse?"

Over the next few years, I asked her these same questions many times. She always answered in a calm, patient voice. She never seemed hurried and was unconcerned that I continued to ask the same questions. She would start her response with: "Of course you want to know. You had what we call a single-incident injury. You suffered brain damage at the time of the assault but more damage will not continue to happen in your brain."

"I'm sorry I keep asking this question."

"You should ask whatever questions you have, as often as you want. I'd like you to take a psychological evaluation so that we can have a baseline now of your cognitive and psychological functioning. Then we'll know the impact of your injuries."

"OK."

The psychological assessment took five hours: batteries of tests to identify where and in what way I had cognitive impairments. In one test I was asked to look at a picture of a block and then replicate the picture with blocks on the table. I couldn't do it. I couldn't even figure out how to start. I tried and then tried again. As the realization sank in—that what used to come easily to me now felt so impossible—I began to cry. Tears flowed. I couldn't remember the five words that were repeated at different time intervals. I couldn't copy a drawing as it became more complex. I was still good at identifying words and knowing the definition of various words. But I didn't need the formal results to know how much I'd changed.

✳ ✳ ✳

Before the seizure, I saw the recovery process as a series of levels to be met. First experience this and master that, then on to the next level. That's how Jean Piaget described cognitive development in children: master one stage and then move forward. I applied this theory to my situation.

In the summer of 2009, I was on medical leave and had increased my level of physical activity and could drive myself to my various therapy appointments. I tied my own shoes and went into stores and cafés, typically trying not to bring notice to myself. I was on my way! After the seizure, though, I needed to find another metaphor to explain and describe my post-assault life. I moved from the image of steps on a ladder to the image of a funnel with no clear boundaries or absolute end points. The funnel does have an aperture that gets wider and lets in more and more light. I needed an explanation of what had happened and a roadmap of what to expect next. A roadmap or guiding theory would help me manage the healing process.

Understanding = moving forward.

Knowledge = more control over healing.

In fact, I could only search for what seemed like rational explanations because I had yet to access my feelings: rage, fear, despair, confusion, and uncertainty. My life's work was built both on my ability to access rational understandings and my skill of empathizing with the emotions of others. The ferocity of the assault smashed my life. Putting the fragments together meant unearthing them from the impact of the battering and from places repressed over a lifetime.

Thirteen: The Permanence of Racism

This is how memory works when being swallowed by terror: it burrows into a brain crevice, a deep hiding place that provides protection from assault. Memory can stay in hiding for an indeterminate amount of time. When memory surfaces, it may have a new shape or form, as if it has been in a witness-protection program. It may still be frightened. Some portions of memory stay submerged, encased in inaccessible places, becoming more unreachable as time passes. Some bits of memory may be revealed quietly, in small portions at a time, and some may thrust themselves into the open and demand attention. Some memories stay lodged in places unreachable by words but reacting only to sensations—smells or sounds—often with no warning. Then they may silently retreat again.

I don't remember talking to the police. The police report contains certain information that I don't recall saying or knowing. Debby received a copy of the police report before I was discharged from GW Hospital. The report itself resembles a school test where the answers must be filled in with a black No. 2 pencil, without going outside the oval, and refers only to the night of January 16, 2009. I have sensory memories, but no specific recollections of my attacker, certainly none that would hold up under a cross-examination, which might go something like this:

Mrs. Jones, how did you know your assailant wore a black sweatshirt and not a navy blue or dark grey sweatshirt? Where there any insignias or logos on the assailant's clothing?

Mrs. Jones, how would you describe your assailant's skin color? Very dark?

The color of this table? The color of your skin? Of my skin? How did you know he was black?

Mrs. Jones, how did you determine that the assailant was male? Did you hear a voice? Did he have facial hair?

I must have said something to the police. Maybe they knew how long it takes memory to find that crevice and so they asked questions before memory had a chance to escape. The official police form reads:

Race: Black

Sex: Male

Exact age or range: UNKOWN

Eyes: Bwn

Hair: Blk

Complexion: unknown

Facial hair: unknown

Hat: Black Hood

Coat/jacket: Black

Pants: Black

Blouse/shirt: unknown

The story of my assault quickly circulated among my friends and members of my home- town and professional communities. Local newspapers carried the story and, since I'm a professor at a local college, the story made the 6:00 p.m. local TV news. My friend Pat, before coming to Washington to be by my side, wrote a beautiful story about me, parts of which were printed in the newspaper in January 2009 and also reported on TV. She referred to me as a white, "anti-racist activist." She wrote:

Let us be moved by what we did not see in Washington on this day (Inauguration Day)—the broken body and damaged spirit of one of our best and our brightest citizens. A college professor and anti-racist activist, JoAnne has spent the past thirty-five years educating students to work for a more socially and economically just world . . . she is a shining example of the "beloved community" about which Martin Luther King Jr. wrote and spoke.

Nothing is race-neutral in our culture. The election of a black president only amplified the already-intense experiences and feelings about race in the U.S. and the thinly veiled white supremacist beliefs that permeate our national identity. This election provided a channel for those who believed that the election might bring forth a real and substantial movement toward racial justice. The election was also a conduit for those to whom the election of a black president was an anathema to their view of America and a clear indication of the downfall of the country.

The language identifying me as an "anti-racist activist" triggered white supremacist websites that troll for such designations. The eloquence of Pat's language and plea for mutual respect was quickly met with vulgarity, hostility, and unvarnished hatred for me and, of course, for President Obama. By the time I left the hospital, there were over ten thousand hits on these websites and blogs. Here are just a few of the postings:

I don't wish for such a thing as this attack to happen to anyone, but if it must happen, then I have to admit I am glad it happened to this subversive, alien piece of filth.

www.thephora.com/forum/ January 28, 2009

As far as the liberal lesbo goes, she got what has been coming to her for years, I suspect. Consider—the woman has preached anti-white hatred for years. She should not be surprised when it goes full circle. I think that some would call this poetic justice maybe. The best part about this is that the nigger [sic] didn't kill her. She gets to sit in the hospital for a while and stew over this in her mind. If she is capable of any rational thought in that fucked up, jewed mind of hers, it won't be long before she changes her ways. If not, then I hope that the next nigger [sic] takes her out.

What a pity the groid didn't anally rape her and use that brick to smash that vulturous shylock face.

www.thephora.com

Almost eight years after these comments were published, many of the blogs, web sites, and journals that used such virulent racist terms in relation about my assault have been repackaged with a cloak of legitimacy with the language of the Alt-Right.

* * *

I grew up learning about race struggles and this country's shameful history toward black people. I learned about Paul Robeson, his talents, and the racist treatment he endured. My parents played the music of Billie Holiday and Bessie Smith and talked about the hardships they and other musicians faced because of race. I heard the stories of Jessie Owens, Jackie Robinson, and Joe Louis. My childhood provided some foundational knowledge and a slight analysis of how racism saturated the history and consciousness of this country.

It was, however, a question posed by one of my professors in undergraduate school that shook up my thinking. He said to the white audience at UC Santa Barbara in the mid-1960s, "If you want to deal with racism, deal with the white community; deal with your own community. That's where racism lives and thrives." This was one of those *a-ha* moments that can give rise to a permanent shift in consciousness. It was the beginning of my realization that the focus of change must first be with oneself, rather than doing for others or attempting to change others.

I had never considered how the racist social structure applied to and implicated me as part of the problem. Gradually, I came to see what had been invisible to me before: I realized that there was only one black student in the college-bound courses at my high school. I graduated from high school in San Francisco. We were a class of five hundred, mostly from working-class families. The numerical majority of students were black, Latino/a, and Asian. I couldn't recall a single teacher of color. We weren't taught about the history of the missionaries in California or the positive histories of non-white peoples. I had friends from different backgrounds, but they weren't enrolled in advanced-placement classes. I didn't notice.

At age twenty-two, I was hired to manage the public welfare program on Kodiak Island in Alaska. It was 1969 and I got the job because I had more education than any other applicant: a bachelor's degree and one year of graduate school in social work. The island was home to a residential treatment facility and school for troubled kids. I quickly saw that *all* of the children in residential foster care were native Alaskans, mostly Aleuts. No one in my graduate program had mentioned that my racial identity might impact how I saw and dealt with these children, but I knew it meant something that I was white and these children came from a culture I hadn't even heard of. What it meant became the focus of my professional career.

My doctoral work and teaching were guided by a race-conscious analysis: making explicit how, in historical and contemporary contexts, race serves to limit opportunities for some and maintain economic and social power for those described by Ta-Nehisi Coates and others as people who think they are white. This was my work; issues of racial justice became my passion. I can't explain why race has been so central to me. I can point to my family background and writings about the affinity between Jews and blacks. Growing up in the 1950s I wasn't seen as white and didn't feel as though I fit into the world of my white, Christian friends. And then there's the enigma of trying to understand why and where a heart travels.

After the assault, my story became intertwined with the most powerful, virulent, and debilitating stereotype in this country: the violent young black man wearing a hoodie. My assault happened three years before the face of Trayvon Martin became the face in the hoodie, the menacing face of a young black man who *could, might, probably was* intent on creating mayhem wherever he was, because that's how "they" are.

Simply identifying my attacker as a "young black man wearing a black hoodie" set in motion an avalanche of stereotypes, myths, and knee-jerk comments. Shortly after coming home, I saw my neighbor, a man in his eighties. He signaled to me to come talk to him.

"I haven't seen you for a few months," he said. "Are you OK?"

"I went to D.C. for President Obama's inauguration and was assaulted."

"Was he black?"

"He was a man."

I was so angered by his comment. All that mattered was race. To say it was a black man explained everything to people like this, and no further conversation was needed.

In other corners of my liberal world, the comments were muted, expressing horror at the savageness of the assault, but with an obvious effort not to linger on the fact that the perpetrator was black. Some wondered aloud if he might have been from the poorest sections of

Washington, or a drug addict needing money, or something else that might help explain such behavior and diminish accountability.

Before the assault, perhaps I, too, would have first considered the background and mental health of someone, particularly a man of color, who perpetrated that kind of violence. I probably would have launched into a macro-analysis, looking at the social context that could explain and, yes, even mitigate an individual action. Now I believe that regardless of my assailant's history, he bears responsibility for what he did to me. He held the hammer. He chose me. He left me to die.

✶ ✶ ✶

Now that some years have passed, I can talk about the intersection of the assault and a host of social factors. In the early years, I had no interest in or ability to intellectualize my experience. While struggling to expose and release the tangle of emotions I felt, I needed compassion and care. I was not a metric, any more than the man who attacked me was the representation of black men.

In my mind, there is no person—no race—associated with the attack. I think only of a shadow topped by a black hood. The hood obscures the face, and the stranger becomes only a hood. My efforts to attach the idea of a real person to the hammer remain abstract. I can describe what I felt and what happened before and since. The assault remains evanescent. It's like trying to catch and hold onto a snowflake. "Black man with a hoodie" is for a police report, a news story, or a conversation intended to confirm that the racial divide continues as the toxic fuel that pilots our culture.

Fourteen: The Balm of Fictions and the Quest for Justice

More than 50 per cent of victims around the world are unhappy about the way police treat them, and many others end up severely traumatized by criminal justice systems, according to the International Crime Victims Survey (ICVS), which has been carried out in more than 60 countries over the past decade.

—Swusthika Arulingam, *Sri Lanka Daily News*, August 17, 2012

I am often asked, "Was he caught?"

"No," I say just as often, adding that catching him will not change my life, that I don't think about revenge or prison, and that I don't think the police have tried to find him.

After the assault, when I was able to focus on TV again, I spent most of my time watching *Law and Order: Special Victims Unit*. I watched the new ones. I watched the re-runs, over and over again. The characters became so familiar; they became my friends. Typically, in each episode, Detectives Elliot Stabler and Olivia Benson identified the perpetrator and, toward the end of the episode, they would save the last person to be abducted or attacked, bringing relief to the victim. They were intensely involved with the case and remained connected to the victims while putting all of their energy into the investigation.

I often fantasized that Benson and Stabler "caught" my case and were appalled by the brutality of the seemingly motiveless crime.

In my fantasy, I meet them for the first time while I'm in the hospital, two days after brain surgery and three days after the assault:

"Hello, Dr. Jones. I'm Detective Olivia Benson and this is my partner Elliot Stabler. May we talk to you?"

"OK."

"We are so sorry about what happened to you. How are you feeling now?"

"It's hard to say."

"We've been assigned to your case and we'll do everything we can to find person who did this to you. We need to ask you a few questions. Answer the best you can."

Olivia then moves toward me and sits on a chair next to the hospital bed. She touches my shoulder gently and then places her hand on the side of the mattress. Elliot sits farther away, as if to give me some privacy in case I share an intimate detail with Olivia, who looks directly at me, her eyes soft and caring, and says, "We've read the official police report and talked to the officers who were first on the scene. We'd like to know anything else that you might remember or even sensed from that evening. Do you remember any smells? The sound of a voice? The feel of material? You were found on your back. Do you remember falling or being pushed? Can you tell us what the weapon felt like? Did the person ask for anything? Can you recall anything?"

"Everything is a blur," I say. "It was all so sudden. I saw my daughter's house and then, I . . . I just don't remember anything else right now."

"You probably feel numb. You're still in shock. We want you to think about these questions. If there is anything, anything at all that you remember, here's my card. Call me right away. We'll stay in touch with you . . ."

They stay involved and call me after I return home. They catch a break when, while investigating a similar crime, they search a suspect's home. They find a cache of presumably-stolen items, including my wallet that still contains my credit cards, driver's license, and forty dollars.

Olivia calls.

Justice.

✳ ✳ ✳

My obsession with *Law and Order* focused only on a victim being saved from terror once the wrongdoer was apprehended. If no one was caught or if the accused was found innocent, I would still find succor because the system was fully engaged in trying to right a wrong. At the end of each episode *I* felt well taken care of. When I thought about the hand that held the hammer, I found neither calm nor peace at the prospect of his capture, prosecution, or incarceration. Getting him didn't matter as much as "the system" *wanting* to catch him—not just any young black *him*, but the *him* who nearly killed me—which would somehow indicate "the system" caring about me. The idea of closure, as in resolution and moving on, puzzled me. I couldn't grasp the notion that everything that I'd experienced would become a vague background to some new, peaceful, and comfortable foreground—this was more than I could imagine.

✳ ✳ ✳

The real detectives assigned to my case never called. The real detectives assigned to my case never even returned *my* calls. No one from the police department ever inquired about my health. After being questioned by police when I was in the emergency room, I was never interviewed again.

I did hear from the woman I called Kind Face from the Victims of Violent Crimes Unit. When the call came, I was in my favorite local women's clothing store in Amherst and out on my own for the very first time since the assault. It was May 2009. The salespeople greeted me warmly. They all knew me. I was browsing, not looking for anything, but just doing something familiar. My cell phone rang. The caller introduced herself but all I heard was, "... police ... violent crimes." *Maybe he's been caught*, I thought. I stood still. My stomach lurched and I heard buzzing sounds in my head. I had to get out of the store fast. I had to focus on this phone call. I went outside, phone pressed to my ear, and walked toward Ren's Mobile Gas Station next door. Ren was always so nice to me. I felt safe near his gas station.

"Pardon me?" I said, trying to get control of my breath.

"We'd like to use some of the pictures of your assault as a training tool," the woman responded matter-of-factly.

I froze.

"They'll only be used for training purposes," her voice lilting now as if she were offering me a one-time, limited special offer.

Pictures. Crime scene. My mind flew back to the alley and I tried to imagine what a camera might have seen. "I have to call you back," I said in a monotone.

I managed to drive home and got quickly into bed. I tried to get my breathing back to a normal rhythm.

I don't know how long it was before I called her back. "You may not use my pictures for any purpose," I said.

In her book, *Aftermath: Violence and the Remaking of a Self*, Susan Brison recounts her life before and in the wake of a brutal rape and assault. She references the experiences of other survivors of human-inflicted trauma and calls into question what "survivor" means in these circumstances. She quotes a survivor of the Nazi death camps: "One can be alive after Sobibor without having survived Sobibor." A Vietnam vet says, "I died in Vietnam," and a rape survivor notes, "I will always miss myself as I was." To be the victim of trauma at the hands of another human is to be reduced to a mere object, a thing, with the stuff that makes one human deemed to be meaningless by the perpetrator. Crime scene photos don't depict *me*. They show blood, grime, swollen, misshapen features, and closed or vacant eyes. But I am nowhere to be found in those pictures. *I am missing.*

After the call from Kind Face, I returned to my nest where I didn't have to deal with anything. I was insulated. My *before* self was buried. The future was no farther than the next TV program, meal, or doctor's appointment.

* * *

The follow-up question to, "Was he caught?" was often, "Was he brought to justice?"

I wanted to say, "Where would that be, this place of justice? Is it when a perpetrator is Mirandized, told his rights and then locked up? Is justice in the courtroom? Is justice in a prison cell? Who benefits when 'justice is done' and the wrongdoer 'pays' for his actions? Will I only have justice if someone is caught, found guilty, and punished for assaulting me? Is being brought to justice like a tax that goes into a pot for the common good and, once collected, allows us as a society to breathe a sigh of relief? *Yes!*, we can say as we exhale. Our system works. We do live in a violent society but now we can move on!"

* * *

In response to the frustrations voiced by victims of violent crimes worldwide, the United Nations agreed, in 1985, to a declaration on the rights of victims:

The right to be treated with respect and recognition

The right to be referred to adequate support services

The right to receive information about the progress of the case

The right to be present and give input to the decision-making

The right to counsel

The right to protection of physical safety and privacy

The right of compensation, from both the offender and the State

(Laura L. Copper, Pursuit of Justice Blog, 9/26/2002)

I was not afforded these rights by the police department.

There was no part of the justice system that helped me to maneuver through and understand my sudden entry into the criminal justice system. I was not treated with respect, nor did I receive information about the progress of my case. I wanted to know: How will the investigation be conducted? What role will I have? How will my family be involved? What kind of information will we be given? How will they stay in touch with me? What happens to someone who is severely injured through random violence? They see this all the time. Maybe it's a too-familiar sight. Maybe Lady Justice is worn out. For me and for my family, our lives were forever changed. What emotional support can they offer? Do they care about us? What words of support can they provide? How can they help me to feel safe again? How does the compensation fund work? Who can I turn to with questions? I needed to be seen and heard by detectives and by the office of the Chief of Police. Why don't I deserve the courtesy of a response from the police and a courteous response from whomever I talk to? Why isn't the PD telling victims how an investigation is conducted? Why aren't they providing useful phone numbers so that I don't have to spend forty-five minutes being transferred from office to office, often retelling my story to receptionists seemingly tired of answering questions? FOIA representatives: why can't I simply get a phone number? And why can't the office of Compensation for Victims of

Violent Crimes at least engage in a single conversation, explain how the fund works and what is available, and if necessary, how to receive additional funds?

I want inclusion in the response to the heinous event that ruptured my world. I don't want to be forgotten or to remain invisible.

* * *

Justice was always a central construct in my life. As young people, and throughout their lives, my parents fought for economic justice. Justice—as seen as a challenge to economic disparities, racism, and xenophobia—was the guiding value in our family.

My work life focused on creating a more economically and socially just world. I wrote about justice. I taught about justice. I believed in justice. It was a grand and spacious concept. When I applied the idea of justice to individual lives, I thought of those mistreated by the criminal justice system: those whose lives were constrained by the many barriers of racism and classism and therefore did not experience racial or economic justice. My relationship to justice involved advocating on behalf of others.

And then I became the victim of violence, and the notion of justice became very personal. I began to see the language of justice, as it encircled violence, as a wrapping that was too eloquent and too ethical—a beautiful and compelling idea that, when invoked, conferred a kind of nobility of spirit on the citizenry. It became clear to me, though, that justice must be entwined with kindness and caring, inclusion and responsibility.

One public official did reach out to me with words of comfort and support: President Barack Obama. I still don't know what process led to the sending of this letter. I know several friends and family members wrote to the White House about the assault and my professional work. Imagine my surprise when this letter appeared in my mailbox, in a plain manila envelope with The White House as the return address.

The White House
Washington
August 21, 2009

Ms. JoAnne Jones
611 South East St.
Amherst, Massachusetts 01002
Dear JoAnne:

I understand that you have been through a difficult time, and I want you to know my thoughts are with you.

We, as Americans, have always drawn on the power of hope, perseverance and faith as we confront life's trials. Although the road to recovery will be long and difficult, I hope you continue to find comfort in the love and support of family and friends and the strength in the principles that guide you.

Sincerely,
Barack Obama [signed in cursive]

The respect and compassion offered so personally by President Obama continues to be a source of comfort and resolve that has helped me to find my way through the difficult years that have followed the assault.

Fifteen: My Voice of Anger

Soon after the assault, a friend, who is also a therapist, asked me to imagine what might have made me feel safer on the night of the assault. She asked me to construct a different story of that evening. I closed my eyes and imagined a Great Dane—named Ampersand—at the scene. I get to the place where the stranger/shadow comes up behind me. I scream and then, faster and quieter than you can imagine, Ampersand jumps the high fence at Rachel's house, dashes toward me, fells the attacker, and holds him with his massive front paws until the police arrive. I'm treated at the scene but have no significant injuries. I continue to Rachel's house with Ampersand by my side.

Even as I tried to engage in this method of dealing with trauma, I knew that I was working hard to make something real that had no traction inside of me. I wished I could have believed in a soothing fable. Ampersand did propel me to think more about having a real dog in my life.

✱ ✱ ✱

When Rachel was ten we got Maggie, a black Lab. After Maggie died, it never seemed like the right time to get another dog. Rachel was in college. My job required a lot of travel and I didn't want to go through the heartache of losing another dog. In the early fall of 2009, Rachel asked me if I felt ready to get a dog again.

Rachel had left her job as a language translator five years earlier to become a licensed dog trainer. She then started her own business training and boarding dogs. She wanted a dog to be my protector, companion, and perhaps be able to detect seizures. I agreed that a canine companion could be an asset to my life.

When I arrived in D.C. for Thanksgiving in 2009, Rachel said, "Meet Rocket." This was the name our grandson Savi had given to the skinny dog that now sat beside Rachel. He was wearing a service dog vest and had short blond hair and ears that stood up like E.T.'s. They looked like antennae. He was funny-looking and already attached to Rachel. I didn't want him. I liked the idea of a dog, but I felt overwhelmed, seeing this real dog. I was becoming rooted in torpor. Rocket would require more time and more energy than I wanted to expend. But since I had given the green light to getting a dog and knew that Rachel would have spent a great deal of time and effort getting Rocket, I accepted him into our lives.

Before she adopted him on my behalf, she'd put him through a series of temperament tests. He showed himself to be a quick learner, eager to please, and very affectionate. Then she brought him to live with her for ten days to see how he interacted with other dogs, new people, and unfamiliar stimuli. He met each challenge without any difficulty. She had him neutered, vaccinated, and ready for adoption. After Thanksgiving, we all drove back to Amherst together to get Rocket settled in his new home.

I don't know when I stopped seeing a skinny, funny-looking dog and saw a beautiful, loyal friend and protector. We spent hours together and he learned quickly. He loved to play, especially running to chase balls. I'd toss a ball from the ball chucker and he'd run so fast he could catch the ball in his mouth before it hit the ground. I'd shriek with joy and he would run back to me, ball in his mouth, and we'd start the game again. Best of all, he loved to cuddle in bed with Debby and me. He would stick his nose under my chin, put a leg on my shoulder and stay like that all night.

I took him with me most of the time. I quickly learned to pay attention to him, interpreting his ears, his gait, and the wag of his tail. On one of our first walks together after he joined our family, I noticed his ears pointing straight up and his nose tilting at about a thirty-degree angle, as if smelling something. I didn't see, hear, or smell anything and continued at my walking pace. He tugged, and the leash became taut. I began to correct him for tugging and then I saw two people walking about one hundred feet in front of me. As they got closer I noticed binoculars hanging from their necks. They were birders looking in the trees and paying no attention to us. I pulled him closer and the walkers went gingerly by us. Through the leash I could feel his body stiffen ever so slightly, alert to the strangers passing by us, though he continued to look straight ahead. After that, I knew to trust his ears, like weathervanes forecasting what lies ahead. I knew to trust his nose, exploring the air for any possible danger signals. I knew I could trust his ability to detect danger before I even had a chance to become startled.

Whenever Debby came home, Rocket would go crazy and rush around the house to find a toy to bring to her. He always had to grab something to give to those he loved. Most of the time it was a shoe. He would get a shoe, run to her car, and wiggle with great force until she could manage to get in the house, put her things down, and let him lick her face.

Rocket was a rescue dog from D.C. He, too, had been traumatized on the streets of Washington. He, too, was hyper-vigilant and cautious. He, too, bore scars—permanent reminders of cruelty done to him. The more I loved him, the more I intertwined our stories. We were both trauma survivors helping each other get through each day. I loved and cared for him. I would talk to him about my feelings. He became my safety net and rapid-alert system.

He protected me in small ways and, as time passed, in bigger and more aggressive ways. In the car: *Grrrrr.* I heard his low growl in the back seat. "What are you looking at?" I said, slightly irritated by his menacing sounds. I turned to look at the man in the car next to us, staring at Rocket and then at me, waving his arms as if to say, "Can't get me."

On the street: "Can I pet your dog?" asked a tall man walking a few steps behind me on the street.

"Pardon me?" I said.

"Can I pet your dog?"

"No. He's not always friendly."

"Oh, I don't care," he said, paying no attention to what I had just said. Then I heard *grrree ruff, grrrrr,* and saw the fur on Rocket's back rise. "Oh nothing," said the man as he quickly crossed the street.

Fuck you, I thought. I still couldn't express my anger, but Rocket was my canine translator.

Now, in my imaginary reenactment of the assault, I'm with Rocket when the assailant comes up behind me and raises his arm. Then Rocket jumps to the height of the hammer, gets the man's arm in his mouth and doesn't let go.

The thought that this *could* be true was of some solace.

Rocket signified a new page in my recovery. I knew I wasn't as strong or as confident as I once was, and I knew there were many feelings always roiling around inside of me. Even with Rocket by my side, I was leery of leaving my cocoon and venturing into places full of noise and questions and sad looks. But now I had a crutch to lean on. I had his love and his growl, his devotion, and his ability to keep others at bay.

I must admit that I got some satisfaction from seeing men give us a wide berth, or cross the street, or look away so that Rocket wasn't alarmed by eye contact. The memory of his love and loyalty to me still gives me pleasure.

In early 2010 I decided to bring Rocket to work with me. He was my best friend. He wore his service dog vest and looked so handsome in it. The vest clearly indicated to everyone that I had special needs. He made my invisible struggles more visible. He could also say, in so many growls, *stay away.*

I took him around to meet all of my co-workers at the college. He let people touch him. I put a special blanket in my office and some toys. I kept him on a leash when the door was open and he stayed on his blanket waiting for me to signal when it was time to move. He wasn't always polite when someone came into my office. He might offer a deep-throated growl or a menacing look to someone he perceived to be an intruder. But he quieted with my stern, "Rocket, down!"

I began to think, again, that I was over the major hurdles. I was climbing up those recovery steps, slowly but surely. I forged through a full teaching schedule from January to April of 2010, gutting my way through the weekends, feeling so proud that I could function in class, be present for students, and respond promptly to their class work and their concerns. After a weekend of teaching and a day or two of grading, I spent the rest of the week in bed . . . exhausted, reconstructing my cocoon and burrowing in.

* * *

April 10 that year was an ordinary day. By then I was finally able to drive myself to work. I noticed the rapidly melting snow signaling the end of winter. There was only one more set of classes in the winter term. I anticipated a more relaxed schedule during the May to August term. I heard my own sigh of relief and self-satisfied chuckle. *Damn girl you're good.* Another hurdle cleared.

We settled into the office, Rocket on his blanket chewing a bone and me sipping coffee as I began to check my email, snail mail, and voice mail. I noticed that I was cc'd on an email from Campus Police to my department chair: "Please advise Dr. Jones that she can no

longer have her service dog on campus because of complaints we
have received. We will require special documentation if she wishes to
bring this dog to campus in the future."

Who had complained? What were the complaints? My Rocket. My
strength.

I closed my office door, wrapped my arms around Rocket's neck,
and wept. He licked my face and seemed to know something bad had
happened.

"Let's go outside for a walk, Rock. Then you can stay in the car and
wait for me until we drive home. OK, good boy?"

Sixteen: Assault Made Visible

I am a minimizer, particularly concerning my own health and mental health. My typical response to most things was "I'm fine" or "I'll be fine." I never wanted the attention of others, nor did I want people doing things for me. Being "fine" was an important standard in my family. When my daughter was quite young and got hurt, I would say, "I bet that smarts." She'd snap back, "It doesn't smart, mom, it *hurts*." And then something of unimaginable magnitude happened.

For months following the assault, I had no thoughts beyond the moment in front of me. It didn't occur to me to think about how my life had changed. To the extent that I sought to understand what had happened, I focused on the science of traumatic brain injury. What was it? What part of my brain was impacted? Would I experience more damage over time? I looked at maps of the brain. I asked the same questions over and over of different medical specialists, trying to master this thing called "traumatic brain injury." I thought that if I could understand it, I could more quickly get to *being fine*.

I read about post-traumatic stress disorder as well. PTSD was even more ephemeral to me than TBI. I could touch my head and feel the gaps in my skull. PTSD existed in a more remote place and, in truth, I thought that I would not be engulfed by it. In my mind, PTSD was the stuff of war veterans, a life-long, never-ending agony following a terrible event. I was embarrassed to refer to myself as traumatized, as if I was usurping the misfortunes of others, making a big deal of something that I should have been able to manage on my own.

I gave little thought at the time to the searing impact of experiencing life-threatening violence at the hands of a stranger. A terrible thing had happened to me, sure, but others had experienced worse. I didn't suffer the insidious long-term damage of domestic violence. I didn't inhabit a war-torn country. I fought against violence but didn't live with it on a daily basis. I was alive. I had a wonderful family. I had a good job and valuable skills. I tried to put the violence done to me at the periphery of my daily life, although I did want people to know that I hadn't had an "accident." I did need to have it known that I was beaten with a hammer. But beyond this telling, I didn't delve more deeply into how the violence had caused another kind of injury, invisible to others but deeply imbedded in my nervous system and my psyche.

✶ ✶ ✶

Given the magnitude of my injuries, I made rapid changes during the first year. Doctors were amazed at how well I looked and functioned. I returned to work; I was regaining my physical strength and the dexterity in my hands. I was indeed doing well. Of course, that was my modus operandi. I was the valedictorian of my high school. *I do well. I succeed. I manage. I move forward.*

During the first year, in 2009, improvement was easy to identify: less medication, more time out of bed, able to take care of my own basic needs, able to drive a car, get on an airplane, and return to the classroom.

Toward the end of that first year, however, the arc of change flattened. Progress was more difficult to distinguish. At first, I was self-conscious about my short hair, visible scars, awkward hands, and unsteady gait. But eventually my hair grew out, I could use my hands, and walk with a steady pace. As these markers of the assault receded, I became more cognizant of the range and scope of injuries that were mostly invisible to others. Every photograph, every glance in a mirror revealed the scarred crevice on the right side of my head. I struggled to tie shoes or open a jar or turn a knob. I was still so very hyper-vigilant. "Watch out," was my constant refrain while Debby was driving the car. I was driving her crazy.

Movement beyond my secure boundaries was still difficult. I tried to refrain from telling Rachel my latest medical treatment and forced myself to start our conversations with, "Tell me what's happening in your life? Did you see . . . ? Are you going . . . ?" I tried to be more of a partner and less of a burden to Debby. "When will you be home tonight? I'm thinking of making a roast chicken. How was work today? Everything in the laundry basket is clean."

But my emotions would erupt without warning.

"WHY ARE YOU CRYING?" Debby implored.

"I went outside and a branch touched my head. I'm so sorry. I'm so sorry. I just can't stop the tears. I'm so sorry."

So many things brought me to tears and so few things bought me joy. Very little was of interest to me. I understood now what it felt like to lose all desire for all things.

My doctors were concerned when I described these reactions and worked to find the right medications to help cushion me. Depression made it hard to even think about how to move beyond the depression. I had never before lived with depression but now had to force myself to interact with others, feeling shrouded in a fog that rarely lifted. I felt minimal pleasure and constant irritation.

"Don't you miss going out, seeing friends, laughing?" Debby asked cautiously.

"No. I don't. It takes too much energy to even consider going someplace. And I don't care. I just don't care."

"Can't you just try?"

"Leave me alone. Please, just leave me alone."

* * *

In 2010, with spring approaching, I could finally sense more light-
ness inside me. Six months had passed since the seizure and I was
driving again. The first flowers of spring had started to push their
way through the ground. The previous spring, I could barely walk
outside, and flowers, which always brought me such joy, held no
interest for me. Now the sight and smell of a crocus was a welcome
reprieve from winter. I started to think about kinds of flowers and
colors for the planter boxes on our deck. I expected a lighter teaching schedule for the summer term, as I had every summer. I thought
about warm days and warm nights and a trip to Cape Cod. Thinking
into the future was a sign that positive changes were finally taking
place inside of me. I was more able to experience and anticipate
pleasure. Six months had passed without a new medical crisis and I
continued to feel stronger. Yes. I was climbing up that ladder out of
the abyss.

I submitted my work plan for the 2010/2011 academic year in
mid-April. I saw the work plan as a perfunctory formality—a yearly
requirement that had never before necessitated prolonged preparation and had never received a thorough review or response. I identified the three classes I wanted to teach during the May-to-August
term, provided an assessment of my teaching, service, and scholarship efforts of the 2009/2010 academic year, and pushed the send
button.

I received an immediate response, by phone. The department chair
informed me that, according to the dean, I had to teach four courses.
I heard his words, received them calmly and assumed that he was
mistaken. I was a tenured, full professor who had held the positions
of department chair, dean, and associate dean. I needed relief from
teaching two full weekends each month, which four courses would

require. I was certain that I knew the rules, policies, and politics of the college. Indeed, I'd had a hand in crafting those policies. I felt emotionally strong and mentally clear.

I immediately sent Joe, the department chair, a memo reasserting that I had always taught three courses in the summer, per the school policy. He reiterated what he had already said. His voice had the emotional tone of a robo-call.

I counter-punched. "Joe! The Americans with Disabilities Act protects me. I need some respite. I'm entitled to reasonable accommodation. I know the rules! I know my rights! I'll talk to the dean." I would learn through this struggle that employers decide what constitutes reasonable accommodation.

I made an appointment to see the dean. No more phone calls or emails. This was personal. Deans can alter faculty schedules. I knew I was entitled. I asked for an appointment with the dean, just to talk.

We met a few days later.

"Come in, JoAnne. It's good to see you."

I entered his office feeling relaxed and self-assured. I sat down at the small faux mahogany, oval conference table in the middle of the room. I smiled.

"Good to see you as well, Bill." He walked toward me and extended his hand. His face was lit by a broad smile. He was a big man and his smile and handshake seemed large as well.

I extended my hand. In my mind we were peers sitting in a room together to work out a common problem. I felt buoyed by the support of my doctors and my administrative acumen. I let my body sink into the chair.

He walked to the opposite side of the table and sat down.

"I'm sure glad I can look out my window and see blossoms rather than heaps of snow," he offered. "I find winters get harder and harder."

I continued the weather conversation. "Do you like winter sports?"

"Used to. Clara and I used to cross country ski a lot. I'm too busy now. I'm happy for a Sunday walk together. What can I do for you today, JoAnne?" His smile wasn't as broad but hadn't yet receded.

"I just wanted to have a conversation with you, Bill. I really don't like writing emails back and forth between me and Joe and you and Joe. For me this meeting is a chance for us to just talk informally. We haven't had a chance to talk together for some time."

"What specifically are you here to talk about?" His smile disappeared. The room felt darker and cooler.

"I talked with Joe a few days ago about my teaching schedule and I know you've spoken to him as well." I moved to the front of the chair.

"That's correct. What was unclear about what Joe told you?"

Now I started reacting to the emotional climate in the room. I felt chilled. I shuddered slightly and moved again in the chair. My head started to buzz and the calm I'd felt morphed into indignation and confusion.

"You know, Bill, you've never even said 'how are you' since I returned to work!"

"Well JoAnne, HIPAA laws prevent me from talking about a personal health condition."

His body seemed even larger.

"Since when did 'how are you?' become a confidential question? A health question?" My voice grew louder. I felt under attack. I tried to quiet myself and then continued. "I'm here because I'm asking for reasonable accommodation to reduce my teaching load in the summer to three courses. I know there are precedents for course reductions."

"You need to teach four courses," he replied in a monotone.

"I didn't hit my head on a copy machine, Bill. I was severely injured. It wasn't a minor 'accident.' I just need a slight change in my schedule. I gave you a list of ten important projects I could take on in place of one class." Now I was incensed, imploring, and embarrassed by my show of vulnerability.

"Are you saying you are not well enough to return to work?" He looked like a hunter who had seen his prey in his riflescope and was now calculating the trajectory of the bullet.

The room was closing in; my head tingled and throbbed. I was trapped and scared.

I needed to flee.

I needed to get out of there as fast as I could.

I simply said, "No Bill, I'm not saying that I can't do my job." I felt trapped. Caught. Nowhere to turn and no one to turn to. "Thank you for your time."

Temperamentally, I have always been reserved and taciturn. Traumatic brain injury had made modulating my feelings difficult. I left Bill's office fuming and muddled. Tears poured from me, as if turned on by a switch I couldn't control. I didn't know what to do. I didn't know how to think about what to do.

✷ ✷ ✷

I reported what happened with the dean to my doctors. They were outraged. They directed me to a social worker who specialized in helping people with brain injuries get workplace accommodations. She too was astonished at how I was being treated, although she added that such treatment is not uncommon. After making a few attempts herself to work with the college, she directed me to a lawyer who focused on getting legal redress for workplace disputes. The lawyer thought my concerns were legitimate and my demands reasonable. I hired her.

I was enraged, but also buoyed by the doctors and specialists who were behind me. They all agreed that I had a solid case. I felt confident in the rightness of my case. I felt justified waging this fight, dander raised, sword *en garde*. I was like a knight charging forward on my trusty steed. I didn't slow down to talk to Rachel who, I'm sure, would have said, "Mom, do you really think it's worth all this time and aggravation?" Debby didn't try to dissuade me from engaging in this battle, though she worried that I would be hurt. I began to imagine prevailing. Maybe getting a reduced workload, permanently, or perhaps a cash settlement to compensate for my pain and suffering. I longed to get justice from *someplace,* from *someone.*

Through my lawyer, I offered the college a long list of tasks I could do in lieu of teaching one course. The dean did not accept any of my suggestions. He didn't offer any comments or make other suggestions. He simply said no. Although he said that he respected my work, and I believe he did, he once again asserted that the steadfast enforcement of policy was essential.

I talked to my lawyer several times a week and sent her stacks of information. I made a list of all the employees I knew of who had received some sort of reduced workload or flexible time schedule. I offered details of academic and administrative functions in need of attention, such as developing a learning center for the school that had grown to encompass eleven campuses spread throughout the country, developing and implementing a more effective advising system, developing online classes, and so on. The college parried my every riposte. I became very weary and decided to let go, stop fighting. I'd simply teach the four courses and end the legal battle.

In response to what I saw as my complete capitulation to the college's demands, they now generated a new demand: I was required to provide medical verification that I no longer had *any* physical limitations. Since a physical disability was the basis of my request for accommodation, if I dropped that request, the college said, I must prove that I was no longer disabled, that I no longer had traumatic brain injury. In effect, I had to disavow any suffering relating to that monstrous event. I had to make it, and myself, invisible.

They did offer one concession: I could reduce my May–August teaching from four to three courses without disavowing that I had injuries from being beaten with a hammer. In return, I had to agree to a salary reduction of $10,000 for that four-month period. I knew it would only take $2100 to hire an adjunct to replace me. I felt battered and defeated.

My lawyer told me to accept their offer. I could continue the fight, but she counseled me that going on would mean more legal fees, and my costs already totaled nearly $10,000. She added that while my concerns were sensible, she didn't think I could win in a court battle. An employer is only required to provide reasonable accommodation and the employer defines what's reasonable. She thought a court would see the salary reduction as reasonable.

I said yes. I stopped struggling. I hung up the phone and started to shake and sob. I was bereft. I didn't have $20,000. I felt like I was back in that alley. Assaulted again. Stricken. Beaten. Powerless. Alone. Defeated. Surprised. Confused. I was humiliated by my hubris at thinking I could prevail and by my show of emotion and vulnerability. My only consolation: this time I knew the face of my assailant. I was, however, not able to protect myself from his violence.

The fog of detachment that had shrouded me for so long now descended again. I felt battered emotionally. My mind kept returning to the corner of Tenth Street and M: Why didn't I walk down Eleventh? I could have prevented the hammer attack if I had just made another choice. If I had walked down Eleventh Street I would not be in this situation at work. It was my fault because I wanted to see the pretty houses. It was my fault because I was so arrogant about negotiating with the dean. It was all my fault.

I had been deftly silenced. I had no metaphors to help organize the boomerang of feelings into a coherent map. I was submersed in a sea of trauma with no horizon in sight.

I decided to call my brother. Our mother had died in October, 2009, and our close connection had become closer during her decline and death at ninety-five. I always called him when something in my life collapsed, and he always responded as my big brother.

✳ ✳ ✳

When I was in the sixth grade, I had to get allergy shots twice a week in an effort to help control my asthma. My parents worked in jobs that did not provide the latitude to take time off of work because of a sick child. It became my brother's task to accompany me on a trek across San Francisco from our home to the Kaiser Hospital Allergy Clinic. He was in high school. He had to take two busses from school to home to get me. Then together we caught the No. 30 express to downtown SF and transferred to the No. 38 Geary to Kaiser Hospital. The shots took a matter of minutes, including the wait, and then we'd repeat the route, although the return meant dealing with rush-hour traffic and crowded busses. He did this for six months until I felt secure enough to make this trip on my own. He wasn't thrilled about having to schlep his kid sister around. We didn't have fun. But he never complained, at least not to me. He was always on time. He never left me alone. I could always count on him to keep me safe. Now, I told him about my predicament and he was concerned for me. Calmly, he said that the problem of money could be easily fixed. He removed the one obstacle he could control. Money was not the only issue, but it was the most tangible one and the one I was focused on. Talking to him, I recognized the old and familiar feeling of his protection. I could breathe.

✳ ✳ ✳

My doctors, therapist, friends, and family told me that my anger was understandable, but that I had to resist feeling responsible for the violence done to me, both in the alley and the workplace. With their help, I was able to halt my descent into despair and self-pity. I had some emotional scaffolding to hold me and, while wobbly, I could continue with work and engage in some facsimile of the ordinary life that I had begun to reconstruct.

It took some time for me to see this episode in a context beyond my despair. I had become the example of what happens when an attempt is made to contravene power brokers. They had time and resources on their side and did not intend to find a compromise agreement with me; rather, their goal was to maintain the status quo, hold on to every dimension of their power, and make sure that the message went out to all: do your job and don't make waves, or this could be you.

Seventeen: You Look Great. Are You All Better Now?

Small step by small step, I rejoined ordinary life. I went grocery shopping and cooked. I went out with friends and traveled to see family. I took medication to keep me awake on the days I taught and medication to help me sleep. I tried to avoid any activity that meant being in noisy settings or being with a crowd of people. I relied on Debby to be my confidant, gate-keeper, and often my spokesperson.

I was often asked, "Are you all better now?" Depending on my mood and ability to exercise self-control, I might give a simple, "Not really," or a more elaborated, "Getting better, but have some ways to go," or "I work very hard to try to get better." At times, though, I might bark that what I live with is *permanent*.

"I have *t-r-a-u-m-a-t-i-c b-r-a-i-n injury and post-t-r-a-u-m-a-t-i-c s-t-r-e-s-s syndrome*," I might say on a bad day, pronouncing each word slowly and carefully so that the full thrust of my injuries were articulated. Debby would sometimes invite someone to feel my head so that touching the deep ravines in my scalp would make it all more tangible.

"My memory is worse and I have trouble with word retrieval."

"Oh, we are all losing memory; remember you're in your sixties! You seem just like your old self; you have your sense of humor," was the unsupportive reply.

✷ ✷ ✷

Other people with TBI speak about how weary they get of paying attention to everything around them and about their shame of constant despondency. They talk about how friends and acquaintances say, "You're lucky to be alive," then adding, "Someone up there is looking out for you."

Susan Brison refers to the disparate experiences of time and recovery. She says, "We impose arbitrary time limits on memory and recovery from trauma: a century, say, for slavery, fifty years perhaps for the Holocaust, a decade or two for Vietnam, several months for mass rape or serial murder." How much time is allowed to recover from a hammer attack?

I had to deal with my own internal conflicts, including wanting to believe that I was *all better now*. I worried that I'd used up my time allotment for recovery and that my suffering was not as terrible as those who live through a war, for instance, or genocide, or long-term abuse. I needed Debby's reassurance that staying home or taking a nap or bursting into tears were all justifiable responses to what I'd been through.

"You look great," was frequently the first comment I'd hear from a friend or acquaintance, whether that person was seeing me for the first time or the tenth time since the assault. Until I learned to just say "thanks," this was the most difficult comment for me to hear.

All of my life, I've been preoccupied by my looks: my Jewish nose. When I was a young child, other kids would ask, "What are you?" I always hoped that they would think I was French. I'd wait to answer, hoping they'd fill in an answer. It was frightening to me to be Jewish, to look Jewish and to be the child of communists. I never really answered the question. I might say Ukrainian because no one knew what that meant. If I thought it would work, I might lie and say, "part Italian." I tried to maintain silence about my family and carried shame about my appearance as if it were an affliction. Oh, to be one of the girls with blue eyes, a pert nose, pretty clothes, and slip-on shoes!

My mother shopped at thrift stores for herself and for me, long before vintage was a "look." I wanted new clothes. I wanted to wear the current fashion. Being considered pretty and having new cool clothes meant being regular. I didn't want to stand out or be different from my peers. As an adult, I love to shop and buy new clothes and new shoes. I have to—at least think I do—look good in order to feel good about myself. If someone gives me a compliment about my blouse or my shoes, I feel attractive for those few moments.

Now I was getting compliments all the time, yet I felt hurt and confused whenever someone said, "You look good."

Even though I knew they meant well, I often wanted to shout, *Look good compared to what? What do you expect—a dithering person with a smashed head? Looking good doesn't mean that the assault didn't happen!* I wanted to tell them that I didn't think or feel like I used to. I wanted to say that loud noises, footsteps, ordinary conversation, and solving problems were all difficult now. Exhaustion blanketed me most of the time. These were the things that no one could see. Also, I couldn't believe that I really looked good—just better than the grotesque image of someone who had been beaten by a hammer. I was torn between the years of being so self-conscious about my appearance and needing, now, to be *visible*. I wanted people to see me from inside, not just the outside. I wanted them to realize that I carried permanent scars, the least of which appeared on my hands and across the top of my head.

With the passage of time, I understood more clearly how difficult it is to offer words of support to someone who has experienced a terrible event. I was able to accept comments with more grace.

Early in the recovery process, Debby captured the conundrum of the vast difference between my external appearance and inside reality:

Caring Bridge: May 2009

It was a nice weekend filled with familiar events. However, I need to remind everyone that it is not the same. On the outside Joanie looks mostly the same, but on the inside she is not the same as she was. This is difficult to say but I feel that it is necessary. It's awkward and more revealing than I normally am, but I am feeling quite protective of Joanie. There are many subtle differences, and some not so subtle. Carrying on long conversations and following the sentences is difficult; concentrating is difficult; loud noise is upsetting; too much can be too much quite easily. Going out is exhausting and challenging, although she is trying to do so. Being spontaneous is nigh impossible and funny things do not seem as funny anymore. Although she looks "good," she doesn't feel good . . .

I think some people feared that my assault might be contagious. If we didn't talk about it, or if we only referenced Washington D.C. as the culprit, or if we agreed that yes, it had happened but was all over now, then we could believe (or make believe) that such a thing could never happen again, or at least never happen "here." Sometimes people didn't know what to say, and in place of "How are you?" substituted "You look good." I remember sitting in a local restaurant having lunch, when a friend or acquaintance would come to my table: "Hi JoAnne! It's so good to see you. Oh, you look great. So great to see you looking so good. Wow. Well, take care." Or, "I know this was a terrible experience for you, but you look great. I'm so glad that you look so good."

Caring Bridge:

I know that the trauma ripples out to all of you who have heard about it and are supporting us through it. That is one of the sneaky things about trauma. The effects can be contagious.

Toward the end of 2010, I was more able to have a conversation where I could listen without having the assault be an invisible presence in the room. With much help, I found ways to stop dwelling on the wrong done to me at work. I tried my best to focus on teaching and on the students, and to keep physical and emotional distance from everything else. Those internalized voices of wisdom also helped me to say a gracious "thank you" when told I looked good. And when I couldn't be gracious, the wise voices told me to say whatever *I* needed to say. I could sometimes go through whole days not followed by the shadow of the assault. I traveled to California alone to see my family. I continued to go to Washington D.C. to see Rachel. Debby and I spent time with friends and each other without the specter of the assault hanging over us all the time. There was some rhythm forming in our lives.

In the fall of 2010, I began to plan my reauthorized sabbatical, which would start in January 2011. At the time of the assault, I had been on sabbatical. I'd had reservations to spend a month on the Bahamian island of Eleuthera. I'd had no fears then of being alone and had relished the idea of new sights and experiences. It was to be an adventure, as well as a way to get my sabbatical project finished: two years earlier I had begun to interview a demographic cross-section of students who were just entering our program. I followed their progress or decline, through interviews and transcript reviews at the beginning and end of each semester. It was a powerful experience and I looked forward to revisiting the experience by rereading each transcript. At the time of the assault, all of the transcripts were packaged carefully in the backpack I carried.

Of course, January 16 had changed everything.

Now I was determined to finally take this sabbatical. I had earned it. All of the research for my project was completed and the sabbatical was to have been my time to write the report. I developed a plan to go to Florida for a month, with Rocket.

* * *

I rented an apartment on Sanibel Island for the month of February 2011. Rachel drove me there and spent the first week with me. Debby came for the last week and then drove me home. It was a grand month. I took long walks on the beach and basked in the sun following several hours of writing. I was surrounded by beauty and comforted by the warm days and nights. Rocket was my constant companion; I loved watching him romp in the waves and leap for balls. He kept a watchful eye on me. Most of the time I was simply "there," thinking about what to make for dinner or whether to walk toward the left or right side of the beach. I didn't seek conversation with anyone other than my family, and the solitary days felt comfortable. I wasn't conscious of being in recovery. I had a simple, mundane, and peaceful everyday life.

That month in Florida served as a template for what I needed to find in my life: warmth, time not infused with stress, activity I could control, a sense of safety, and interaction with others that was supportive instead of intrusive. I needed to find ways to bring Florida into my everyday world. My time in Florida helped me realize how in so many ways I had become like brakes with no pads—metal on metal—or knees with no cartilage where bending causes damage and great pain. My reflexes did not send me into problem-solving mode, as they once had, but rather into survival mode, calling on body memory and cortisol in another fight for survival.

It was suddenly clear that I needed to retire. I was approaching 65 and needed space and time. I needed to build the psychological muscles that could help me move with more ease through each day, not simply persevere. The night before I left Sanibel, Rocket and I walked along the beach to watch the sun set. I was uplifted by the metaphor of a setting sun, as one day ended with another soon to begin. A clear and energizing plan took shape. I was required to work for one year following sabbatical leave. I would give my notice at the end of 2011 and formally retire in August 2012.

"Let's go home now, Rock, and celebrate. I'll have a glass of wine and I'll give you a fresh marrow bone." I didn't know yet that there was more trouble again that would heap more sorrow on our lives.

Eighteen: Dueling Traumas

I was always careful about where I took Rocket. That spring, I knew he was becoming more territorial. He had started to lunge at the ankles of cyclists, once getting his mouth on a woman's shoe. He began to growl at runners and snarled at anyone who passed our house. His fur stood up when he was near other dogs. "I can handle him," I insisted when Debby raised concerns. "I'm just not doing all the things I need to do. I need to watch more carefully and spend more time training him. He's fine. Stop worrying."

On a rainy spring morning in May of 2011, I went to a nearby conservation area that allowed dogs to be off leash. I kept him leashed, but at the end of our walk I took him off the leash. There were no other cars in the parking lot. The only person I'd seen all morning was a runner on the other side of the river. I let Rocket wander upstream as I looked for river rocks to use in our garden.

"Fuck! I'm being bitten." I looked to my left to see Rocket's mouth on a man's calf. I called Rocket and grabbed him.

"Jesus fucking Christ. Fuck. Fuck," he yelled.

"I'm so sorry," I said, my heart pounding, Rocket now sitting at my side. "Are you OK?"

"OK? Are you fucking kidding? Do you have a cell phone?"

"Yes. It's in my car. I'll go and get it."

"No way! I'm not letting you out of my sight."

We walked single file toward the parking lot about fifty yards away. He continued to shout: "What if my child was with me? What if this dog bit a child? If he did I'd kill him with my bare hands. I'll make sure he never hurts anyone else. I'll make sure he's put away. What kind of person are you? This isn't the dog's fault. It's you. It's you. It's your fault. You should never have a dog. Do you think this is funny? What's wrong with you?"

My breathing became labored. I heard his words and I noticed the parking lot. I felt like I was looking at the horizon on a long drive. What I saw in front of me seemed endless and out of proportion. A few yards stretched on; I saw my car but nothing else in the parking lot. His words reverberated like an echo, coming in and bouncing back.

When we got to my car, I put Rocket inside, took out my purse with my phone and driver's license and called 911 to report what happened. We were both standing. I felt like I was epoxied to my car.

"You probably didn't make the call at all. Why are you so nonchalant?" He wouldn't stop shouting.

"I'm horrified that this happened." I could barely hear my own voice.

"Hey Sally, do you have a cell phone?" he called to someone on the other side of the parking lot.

I felt numb, unable to move. I didn't know what to do. Knowing what to do in difficult situations had always been one of my strong suits. I could think clearly, make decisions, keep a situation from becoming more volatile and give a measure to comfort to others. That was *before*.

As he walked away to use his friend's phone, I tried to call Debby. I couldn't reach her. I called Rachel and started to cry as I told her what had just happened. I couldn't stop the tears and I couldn't move from the car door. Rachel was calm and reassuring. She told me to make sure to mention how abusive this man was to me.

The animal control officer and an ambulance arrived at the same time. The officer, Cheryl, came over to me and wrote down my story.

Rocket was barking at her from inside of my car. The man walked up to her, still yelling and making threats about what he thought should happen to Rocket and to me. He then walked over to the ambulance. Five minutes later he exited the ambulance. He had a puncture would that required antibiotic ointment and a bandage. He was advised to see his doctor, just to be thorough.

He walked toward me again and Cheryl moved and stood between us. She told him to back away and assured him that she would take care of everything. I was still crying. He started to walk away and I heard myself say, in a barely audible voice, "Will you tell me your name?" He walked a few steps more, turned, and spat his name at me.

I was, of course, horrified that Rocket had bitten someone. I was mad at him and needed him at the same time. As he looked out through the car window, daring anyone to come close, I just wanted to be inside of that car to calm him, to feel his fur, to be comforted by his love for me. We were like two halves of a catamaran, each unable to navigate without the other.

After that day, I couldn't really remember what the man looked like and recoiled whenever I saw any man with grey hair of a certain height. He became another faceless threat. I became cautious again of going into familiar places. What if he was there? I flinched if I heard the sound of any man speaking loudly or shouting, for any reason. If someone raised a voice at me or questioned me, I would either crumble or respond explosively. In my mind he was now entwined with the hooded shadow and the dean.

I still needed to handle the tasks of everyday life. Rocket and I still spent most of our days together, although I had to find places to walk him isolated from runners, hikers, and bikers.

In October of 2011, I received notice from an attorney informing me that I was being sued by the man for loss of half a day's work and for a lifetime of trauma resulting from the dog bite. A lifetime of trauma! How dare he? How dare he trivialize trauma? He had no idea of the impact of his behavior on me. I was enraged once more. I called my insurance company and railed about the man and his lawsuit. The patient person on the phone told me that dog bites are always considered the fault of the dog owner. He said he sympathized with my story but could do nothing, although he added that the insurance company waits for a year or so to see if there really is a long-term health problem or if a bite mark is still visible. I wanted to write a letter and tell him about what had happened to me and how his behavior had re-traumatized me. I would tell him! But I didn't. The lawsuit faded away, as did the bite mark.

Soon after receiving the notice that I was being sued, Rocket frightened another runner with a menacing bark. The runner tripped and fell to the ground. The incident was reported to animal control. It was Rocket's second strike. Dogs in my area only get two chances; his time had run out.

The day when I was told that we could no longer have Rocket, I thought my whole world had collapsed. I called Rachel, again putting her in the care-taking role. I blurted out that Rocket had to come and live with her. I didn't ask her first or think about the impact on her life. I couldn't admit that Rocket was becoming more aggressive. I didn't think. I was flooded with feelings and frozen. All I could do was cry and turn to Rachel for help.

✶ ✶ ✶

At the end of October, I decided I needed to be alone with Rocket before taking him to live with Rachel. I had begun to think about writing about the assault and its aftermath. I reasoned that a trip to the Cape would give me the time and space to write, and I knew I'd be safe with Rocket.

I'd been going to Truro almost every summer for twenty-five years. I loved Truro. I used to imagine going there in the off-season.

I'd wear an ivory cable-knit wool sweater for walks on Long Nook Beach. I imagined huge waves pelting the shore and a cold wind circling me. Then I'd return to my small cabin, perched on a hill overlooking the sea, where I would write. I didn't consider what I'd write, but the view and the sweater were clear images.

I found a very, very small cottage, nestled in a grove of identical cottages. From the windows, I could see the adjacent cottages, although only one other was occupied at the end of October. The cottage measured about 400 square feet. The kitchen section had a stove, refrigerator, sink, a small counter that served as a food preparation area, plug-in for coffee and toaster, and eating space. Immediately adjacent to the kitchen was a space with two funky overstuffed chairs, a small TV, and a coffee table. Along one wall was a bookshelf, lined with mysteries left by various past guests and the ubiquitous summer-cottage Scrabble game. The chairs and coffee table could be moved to lower a murphy bed, which, once in place, scarcely left room to walk. I unpacked my clothes and put away the food I brought. I pulled the Murphy bed down and our nest was ready.

Each morning, we went to Long Nook Beach. The combination of cold weather and few tourists meant the beach was empty, and Rocket could be off leash and run. He loved to chase his mountain drool toy, a plastic squeaky toy shaped like the soda Mountain Dew. I'd throw the toy in the waves; he would dash after it and bring it to me for another round.

We'd repeat the same routine at night. After dinner, I joined him on the Murphy bed and tried to find reruns of *Law and Order*.

✶ ✶ ✶

The tiny space, blustery October weather, and the somberness of knowing that Rocket would soon leave my life provided a quiet, introspective atmosphere for writing. After our morning walk and breakfast, I would sit on a stool at the table/counter with the wind howling outside, Rocket comfortably positioned on the Murphy bed, his ears pointed up and his eyes fixed on the door. I would check to make sure he was all right and then close my eyes and start to write. I wrote only about the time just before the assault, that moment when it happened, and my first days in the hospital. With my eyes closed, those scenes replayed and replayed like a homemade video stuck on repeat. I wrote what my mind saw.

I'm not sure what generated this strong urge to write. I had written random thoughts about the assault from the time I was able to use my hands. These were mostly rants that I didn't want to share with anyone. Debby in particular encouraged me to write a book, but I saw it as a crazy suggestion. Writing a book seemed like a huge undertaking and I no longer saw myself as someone who took on big projects. I now saw myself as limited. Yet the thought continued to percolate.

Each day the writing followed the same pattern: I'd close my eyes and go back in time . . . *Shop for warm clothes, go to Bradley airport, buy the donut and coffee, board the U.S. Airways flight and take my window seat. Ride the metro. Walk down Tenth Street, and descend into hell.* I wrote about my memory of giving the EMTs Rachel's number, waking up in the ER and then the ICU. I wrote about the same scenes, adding some words, taking out some words and sometimes changing the order of a few paragraphs. A rhythm for writing emerged surprisingly quickly. My hours of writing were meditative. Other than a banging screen door, I was surrounded by silence. Pictures entered my mind and were then recorded with my fingers.

I left the cottage without Rocket once, to walk up and down Provincetown's Commercial Street. Most shops were closed and only a few restaurants were open. It felt odd to be in a place at once so familiar and now eerily different. A passing car or a bicycle replaced the raucous street sounds of summer. After an hour, I decided to buy some take-out food and return to the cottage and Rocket.

I didn't worry that writing about the moment of the attack over and over again would sear this horror into me like a tattoo burned on the inside of my skin, painful and seemingly unreachable. In that small space, alone and safe, I allowed whatever was inside to empty onto a blank page. I was the scribe for my amygdala. I didn't think about who might read it. I didn't think about how the writing might impact me. I let go of worrying about the damage to my frontal lobe and allowed the wild part in me, terrified of dying and desperate to survive, to do the writing.

When the week ended, I was satisfied with my first step into writing. To my surprise, I'd been able to concentrate and had the discipline to follow a daily schedule. I'd spent hours each day engrossed in recreating the experience that changed my life. Words and images had come to me and I'd been able to capture them on paper. I didn't know where this writing was going, but I knew I had made a real start.

Once we returned from Cape Cod in late October, Debby and I drove Rocket to Washington to live with Rachel. I stayed for a week before returning home. When I left, he also became aggressive toward other dogs. Rocket was strong and very fast. With no provocation, he began to bite dogs—small ones, big ones—severely enough to break the skin and cause injury. He couldn't return to Amherst. He couldn't stay with Rachel. We would have to immediately find someplace where he'd be away from other dogs and with limited or no contact with people. He couldn't go back to the animal shelter. We made the excruciating decision to put him to sleep. It fell to Rachel to make it happen. She found a veterinarian that would come to her house. With his head on her lap and eating contentedly from a bag of his favorite kind of cheese, Rocket passed quietly.

Nineteen: A Claw-Foot Hammer and a Black Hoodie

I t is hard for most people to sit comfortably with the reality of random violence. You can walk down the street, turn left rather than right, and be bludgeoned by a stranger for no reason. It can happen in a café, a school building, or on a bus. It can happen anywhere, anytime, to anyone. There is no warning, there is no protection, and there are no limits.

I knew the sudden horror of major national calamities, like the assassination of JFK and the destruction of the World Trade Center towers. But before the assault, I hadn't known random violence in an intimate way. After it happened, I still couldn't grasp that a stranger had come up behind me and, without saying a word or asking for anything or making a demand, beat me with a hammer. He took my purse. He dropped it two blocks away with my money still in a bank envelope alongside a bloody claw-foot hammer. Even as I live daily with the consequences of this bizarre story I wonder, was this real?

The arbitrariness of my assault was also mystifying to everyone else in my world. I could see listeners cringe as I told the story. So unbelievable! It was a subcategory of random, the *random unbelievable*. Sometimes I would stare at a hammer and think it just wasn't possible for someone to have used it to bash in my head. There were often moments when it seemed so surreal to me. The random assault of a stranger with a hammer happened on crime shows. How was it possible that it really happened? That *I* was the victim?

✷ ✷ ✷

Just after I returned from a trip to California in the spring of 2012, I received an email from a good friend in San Francisco saying that she had just heard a startling story on a local radio station about a man arrested in Washington, D.C. for allegedly beating several people with a hammer. It became news in California because the person arrested, Michael Davis, was the younger brother of a player for the San Francisco 49ers.

I was stunned. I had heard nothing on my local or national news, but I immediately started researching the story. This is an excerpt from an article that appeared in the Washington Post on April 27, 2012:

> *After a man was killed and two other people injured in separate attacks in the District's Petworth neighborhood this week—each victim apparently chosen at random and struck on the head with a weapon—police saturated the area Thursday night with officers in plainclothes and unmarked cars. They feared a serial assailant was at large. The tactic bore quick results.*
>
> *Some of the officers, patrolling in the 800 block of Gallatin Street NW about 9 p.m., heard a woman scream for help. Like the earlier victims, she had been grievously injured by a sudden blow to the head. As the officers rushed to her aid, police said, they noticed a man with a backpack staring at them from an alley.*
>
> *When the officers stared back, police said, the man turned and ran. Minutes later and a few blocks away, after a frantic*

foot chase ended with the suspect in handcuffs, officers opened his dark-colored backpack and peered inside.

Just hours into what might have become a protracted hunt for a dangerous and unpredictable attacker, police said, they caught a key break: They found a claw hammer.

My heart sank. I read and reread the story.

"Apparently chosen at random"

"Struck on the head with a weapon"

"Fear serial assailant at large"

"Grievously injured by sudden blow to the head"

"Found a claw hammer"

I just knew it had to be the same man who assaulted me. The story was the same. Sudden attack from behind. Chosen at random. Serious injury. HAMMER.

The story of these attacks in Washington, in a neighborhood only three or four miles from Rachel's house, gave a new reality to my experience. I wasn't hallucinating. I felt an odd and deep kinship to these strangers. I wanted to meet them, to call to see how they were doing. My heart broke for the man who was killed and I was reminded that I could have died as well. I always thought that whoever attacked me would attack others; it didn't seem likely that such an assault could only happen once. The police suspected a serial attacker. It MUST be the same assailant. So similar in the location, the description of the perpetrator, and the weapon used. Now I would have a face and a name and maybe some answers.

After the newspaper articles appeared, two more people in the Petworth area came forward to say they too had been attacked, although they did not have serious injuries. They saw their attacker and gave a description that fit the person in police custody, a young black man wearing a dark hooded sweatshirt.

I immediately called Detective No. 1. He had been assigned to my case. I wanted to know if he was trying to link my case to this recent spate of hammer attacks. I was told he was gone for the day.

"When will he be back?"

"Tomorrow at three p.m. He'll be here for the night shift."

"Thank you."

I called at three the next day.

Again he wasn't there. He was already "out on the streets."

I called again and, when told he wasn't there, I realized that there was no point in waiting to talk to him; I could talk to any detective.

The next time I gave the phone to Debby. Just the thought of talking and retelling my story made me cry.

She told our story to Detective No. 2, who answered the phone. He said that Detective No.1 was also working on the hammer cases and would call us back.

He didn't.

I called again and talked to yet another detective (No. 3). I told him the story. He was soft-spoken and was so sorry this had happened. He would tell Detective No. 1.

But I never heard from Detective No. 1, No. 2, or No. 3.

I got angrier and angrier. All I could think about was this case and my certain knowledge that there was a link to me. The person who assaulted me was in custody and I wanted, I *deserved* answers. Don't shut me out! Don't leave me alone! Getting answers gives me visibility. Please!

I called the office of the chief of police. This time I got a call back within an hour from Detective No. 4. He was pleasant and said he had read my file.

"This isn't the same person," he said. "In your case, it was a robbery. There are details I can't tell you, but it's not the same person," he said with no inflection in his voice.

"How is that possible? I wasn't robbed," I yelled. "He left my money, $400.00. He hit me with a hammer. How many hammer attacks happen in Washington, D.C? Are you even trying to see if there is a link?"

"Well ma'am, we'd like to have more charges against this person who's been arrested. If there is a link we'll let you know."

I became certain that the police couldn't draw a link between the Petworth incident and what happened to me because they didn't process the evidence. The more I seethed, the more I began to suspect that the police had done nothing in relation to my case, including a forensic analysis of the bloody hammer. They weren't talking to me now because they were covering up their own malfeasance. I was sure of it.

My next tactic was to ask for my files through the Freedom of Information Act (FOIA). I would discover their cover-up.

I researched the process, talked to a lawyer friend, and sent in my written request. The FOIA guidelines indicate that a response to a query must be made within ten days. On the tenth day after submitting my query letter, I received an email stating that because of the amount of the information I requested, a reply would take longer. I noticed that the same person to whom I addressed my original request did not sign this email.

I waited. After a month, I called the FOIA representative for the MDCPD. She told me that the person I wrote to initially and the individual who signed the email notification to me no longer worked there and that she would get back to me. I waited. I called again. Now I spoke with yet another person. She informed me that she had found my request in the computerized records but could not find my file.

Now I was sure there was a conspiracy. I began planning my next steps. I'd contact the reporter in D.C. who covered these attacks and the reporter in Colorado who wrote about Gary Dederich—the man who was killed, allegedly, by Michael Davis. I wouldn't deal with the police. I was going public with this scandal.

Rachel tried to tell me that all of this ruminating would not benefit me. Though she agreed that the police were deficient in their response to me, she didn't think there was a conspiracy afoot.

In the midst of my strategizing, I received a call from the newest FOIA representative. She apologized for all of the delays and told me that she was mailing the police report and a CD of other information pertaining to me. Some information, she said, could not be provided.

The official letter from FOIA was dated November 16, 2012 and began with the list of my requests. In addition to specific reports regarding my case, I asked for:

Any record of other investigations where the victim was attacked with a hammer or an attempt to rob with a hammer was made;

Any collateral investigation or contacts relating to my case; and

Records requesting forensic testing of the evidence and the results of the forensic testing that were done in relation to the investigation of this case.

The letter from FOIA notes:

"After due consideration, your request is granted in part and denied. Please find attached a copy of an Incident Report, Evidence Report, and Supplementary Evidence Report with attachment of a sketch and a copy of a CD containing photos.

"With regard to any and all other outstanding documentation or information you have requested, please be advised this is an open investigation and release of such information would interfere with law enforcement proceedings pursuant to D.C. Official Code #2-534(a)(3)(A). Once additional information becomes available it will be released to you accordingly."

Debby was the only one home when the envelope arrived. She opened it and started to look at the enclosed CD. Then she stopped. The images were too hard to see. They were the crime scene photos of my battered head, blood-soaked clothes, and pools of blood in the alley. They were pictures taken of me in the emergency room, head bloodied, eyes closed and swollen, neck held in place by a cervical collar, and hands misshapen.

She hid the CD. I've never seen it.

✶ ✶ ✶

My investigative focus turned toward the prosecutor's office. I wouldn't deal anymore with the police or bureaucratic offices. I wanted to know how the ADA's office was handling Michael Davis's case and to make sure they knew about what I was sure was additional evidence from my case. I wanted to know who was handling the case from the district attorney's office. I knew he had been arrested in the third district. I called the number listed online for courts handling felonies in the third district.

"Hello. My name is JoAnne Jones. I'd just like some information, please. Can you give me the name and phone number of the ADA handling the Michael Davis case?"

"You'll have to call the Superior Court office. They have all of the ADA names."

"Thank you."

✶ ✶ ✶

"Hello. My name is JoAnne Jones. I'd like some information please."

"We don't give out the names of ADAs."

"I understand. I was assaulted in 2009 and I believe there is a connection with a current case and I'd just like to talk with the ADA assigned to this case."

"Oh. You need to call Civil Court. I'll transfer you."

"Thank you."

"Hello, my name is JoAnne Jones. I was told that you can give me information about the recent hammer attacks . . ."

"You need to call Superior Court."

"I just did!"

"Well, you need to call again. I'll transfer you."

"Hello, my name is JoAnne Jones . . ."

Sigh. Sigh again, louder. "You just called. I told you what to do."

"I keep calling. I've been calling for over thirty minutes now. I just want a phone number."

"I'm sorry. I have already given you the information." She hung up.

I was now so angry. I decided to call every number listed on the DC Court web page.

"HELLO. ALL I WANT IS A PHONE NUMBER. I was beaten with a hammer a few years ago. I can't get any help," I repeated as soon as my call was answered.

"OK." I finally heard. I was taken aback. Then he said, "Can you give me some more information? What is the name of the defendant? I'll check my files. OK, the name of the prosecutor handling this case is . . ."

I sat cradling the phone next to my ear. I would call the prosecutor soon enough. Now I wished I had asked for the name of the young man who gave me the phone number—the young man who finally listened, heard my anguish, and responded to me.

I spoke to the ADA. He listened patiently to my questions, though couldn't provide the answers I wanted. At the end of the conversation he said, "I'll have the homicide detective handling this case call you."

Within an hour, the detective called. He sounded sympathetic to my yearning for information. "I'm sorry, ma'am. The truth is, we would not have been able to catch the person who assaulted you unless an officer had been in the alley at the time. Please call if you have other questions."

✳ ✳ ✳

Michael Davis has been in court several times over the past years. Each time he has been found not mentally capable of standing trial. He has been in a mental health facility since 2012.

I was on a fool's errand in my quest for unequivocal knowledge. I thought that if I knew exactly what was happening in my brain, if I knew what parts of my frontal lobe were impaired, if I knew precisely what had happened to my head during the assault, if I knew why he did this to me, if only I could understand, then I'd be better able to cope.

My quest for information did yield some results. I became more knowledgeable about brain functioning, TBI, PTSD, and the criminal justice system. The links between feeling better and acquiring more details were tenuous, though. When I received something from the police, I wanted more. When I learned more from my doctors, I wanted to know about the future. What might happen? Tell me what specifically is happening now. Then tell me what *will, might, could* happen in the future. My needs were never sated.

Twenty: End of an Era

In the late spring of 2012, over three years after the assault, I started to disassemble my office and my work life. I was in the countdown to retirement. After I submitted my retirement letter in October, I began to make lists outlining how many more faculty meetings, how many more classes, and how many more trips in total would I make to the college until August 31, 2012. Each week I would recalculate. Then it was time to stop counting days and start actively dismantling the tangible pieces of my work life: the files, the boxes, and the bookshelves.

I started with the filing cabinets, throwing out minutes of meetings long since passed and policy statements of policies no longer in effect. I threw out manuals, memos, and annual faculty handbooks. I threw out budget reports and enrollment reports. I threw out reams and reams of paper with words and numbers that once seemed so important.

While heaving everything into a large garbage can, my mind drifted to the beginning days of my work.

I could recall so clearly the day I was told that I'd been selected for the job of associate dean. Our school had just merged with the college. We were now a component of the college, but with a significantly different class schedule and curriculum format. The merger was a bit like trying to find common ground in the music, values, and appearances of Pat Boone and Bob Dylan. My team was trying to catch answers that were blowing in the wind. The other team took great pride in their core Christian values and their belief in American Exceptionalism. It took many years to find some harmony.

＊＊＊

The garbage can filled with paper. I went in search of another.

In my take-home box, I only put the books I'd used in teaching. The rest went into a give-away pile. I picked up Dorothy Allison's *Bastard Out of Carolina* to place in the bring-home box. It was the first book I'd chosen for the class "Women's Issues through Literature," a course I co-taught for sixteen years with my dear friend and colleague Camille. We designed the course so that student presentations took place on the last day of class. The assignment was to offer a synthesis of what was learned from the course that included both class materials and personal reflections. Most of the presentations were amazing, but I'll never forget one in particular.

As always, there were tables laden with food for the end-of-class potluck. Pulled pork. Rice and beans. Meatballs. Collards. Flan. Mac and cheese. Chicken wings. Salads and drinks. The student giving the last presentation used the song "I Will Survive" as the focal point of her talk. She began by describing what the song meant to her, giving anecdotes from her life and references to the books we read in class and the theories we had discussed. She talked about the lyrics and the role that music has played in her life. We all listened patiently. At the end of her formal presentation, she played the version made popular by Gloria Gaynor. We all knew the lyrics. It had become a rallying cry for women everywhere. After the first stanza, everyone stood and began to move to the beat. Soon we were holding hands and winding our way through the classroom, our raucous voices almost drowning out the music. Then the classroom door opened and in came the group in the classroom next to ours, snaking through the door, dancing and singing, hands held high. We formed one long line and danced our way into the hallway, proclaiming our determination to survive, as long as we had love.

Back then, I did not think of myself as a survivor. I understood the song as paying homage to the strength of women. Most of the students in that class had experienced sexual, emotional, and physical abuse. They knew struggle and they knew how to find joy in the midst of that struggle. I loved the song and I treasured these women who taught me so much.

* * *

As I sat in my office now, the words came spilling out.

Oh no, not I, I will survive

Oh, as long as I know how to love, I know I'll stay alive

The sound of my own voice brought me back to the papers and books piled around me. I could still feel the profound joy of joining my voice to the voices of the other women in that classroom.

During my final weeks of teaching, I was determined to enjoy what I loved the most—the classroom. In class I could be in the present moment. I always brought food into each class. The day was so long, and food created a comforting and inviting space. We engaged in animated conversations, laughed a lot, and ate a lot; students also talked about the impact of my teaching and offered their hopes for my health and wellbeing in retirement.

"I'll hold you in my prayers, Dr. Jones. "

"Thank you so much for sharing your experience. Something similar happened to me. I had just gotten out of the shower. There was a man standing in the door. I screamed and grabbed a towel. I pushed him and ran into the street. I was screaming and screaming. Someone called the police. They caught him running through the neighborhood. I never told anyone. Not even my boyfriend. I felt so ashamed like I had done something wrong. You're the first person to know this story. Can I hug you?"

"You're so brave to talk about what happened. Thank you."

"Most professors never share something personal. Hearing you makes me feel stronger."

"You've changed my life . . ."

There were many kind and generous words of support as well as flowers, gifts, and of course, offerings of food.

"I heard you like flan so I made flan for our last class."

"This is my mother's special rice and beans that she made for you. I told her about you. She sends her love and hopes you like the food . . ."

✶ ✶ ✶

Following the assault, work, which had always been a source of vitality for me, had become draining and too often re-traumatizing. But these final months helped reignite my love affair with teaching. I was able to stop thinking about being tired and to feel the tingle when course readings kindled animated discussions, often with several people talking at the same time, each unable to wait. At the end of each day, alone in my office, I felt so satisfied, so proud of myself. With everything that had happened and was still happening, I was still a skilled, compassionate educator with a great sense of humor. I still had it!

I decided to take control over external events—in particular, how I would conclude my formal relationship with the college.

The college always hosted a reception for retiring faculty where the dean of the retiree's school offered a glowing speech, followed by the presentation of a gift, typically a chair etched with the college's logo. After receiving the invitation to my reception, I told the dean that I could not attend.

"You'll say flattering words meant only for a public performance. I didn't survive in order to be a hypocrite," I wrote him.

He responded by offering the words he would have said and assuring me that they were authentic. I didn't respond to him or go to the reception, but I did receive the chair through the mail.

I now spoke openly at faculty meetings, in private offices, and in gathering places—like the lunchroom or around the copy machine. I talked about how, through my new understanding of trauma, I could see the erosion of self-confidence and a heightened sense of fear in my co-workers from the quiet mumbling between people when they thought it was safe to talk out loud.

As my parting act, I decided to invite myself to have an exit interview with the provost. I wanted to be explicit about how the college had responded to the horror that had happened to me and I wanted to describe what I saw as ongoing workplace violence and hostility. And I wanted to tell my own story about my recent history with the college and use my own language in the telling. I *needed* to speak, but did not need or expect a response from the provost.

On my way to the provost's office, I completed my final obligations, turning in my office keys, my computer, and my parking pass.

I entered the office that I'd been in so my times during the tenure of five previous incumbents. The room remained basically unchanged over the years except for the personal memorabilia on walls and furniture tops. It was a spacious room. A large mahogany desk was centered in front of tall windows facing the college's manicured quadrangle. There were two chairs in front of the provost's desk. A coffee table was placed in the middle of the room, low enough to be casual and large enough to accommodate papers for a meeting. Upholstered chairs ringed the coffee table.

I entered the room. She greeted me and motioned for me to sit in the informal seating area.

The conversation went roughly like this:

"It's good to see you, JoAnne. Are you excited about your retirement?" She extended her hand to me.

"Yes. Very much so. How are you, Doctor?" I asked. "I know you've been

ill recently."

"Thank you for asking," she said, head nodding.

A few seconds passed. Nothing more was said. I continued.

"I made this appointment because I have some serious concerns. I don't expect answers. I only wish to be heard. We haven't had the opportunity to speak directly during your time in this position." (I omitted the fact that she'd been in the position for ten years.)

"You're one of the old-timers with your school, aren't you? How long have you been here?" She said nothing about the fact that we'd never had a conversation.

"Yes, I'm an old-timer. I've been here for twenty-five years. I've loved my job. Loved the students and have had the opportunity to be a part of all aspects of our school's functioning. I've also had the opportunity to be part of college and trustee committees. But right now, I'll just talk about my experience in the recent past. I do want you to know that many people share my perception that our school feels emotionally toxic."

I provided a brief synopsis how the administration had responded to me following the assault.

She remained still. Her expression seemed painted on her face. I continued.

"I returned to work two days after having a seizure. My attention to students never wavered but there were certain things I couldn't do, like drive. My colleagues came forward to offer rides and assistance."

Now she responded very quickly. Her jaw became more set, jutting out as if she was giving directions by pointing her chin. She had the demeanor of someone greeting people at a cocktail party: friendly, detached, and doing a necessary but not particularly pleasant chore.

"Isn't it wonderful that we work in a community where people offer that kind of help?" She smiled slightly as if reaching for a canapé while finding something of common interest to say to the disagreeable stranger at the cocktail party.

"Thanks for your time," I said as I stood up to leave her office.

I didn't expect anything from her, and I didn't get anything. I did get the satisfaction of saying what I wanted to without hesitation or apology.

* * *

I walked into the warmth of a bright August day. The campus quadrangle was covered with lush green grass and bordered with beautiful flowers planted in orderly, color-coordinated rows. I got into my car and drove away, never looking in the rear-view mirror.

Once home, I did what I typically do after too many hours in the world: I climbed into bed and turned on the TV. I probably watched an episode of *Law and Order: Special Victims Unit*.

Twenty-One: Divine Canines

In late August 2012, a week before my formal retirement date and almost a year after Rocket died, I received a call from my stepson, Robbie. His girlfriend Maria had just started to work as a personal care attendant for woman who was confined to a wheelchair. While in Maria's care, the woman died suddenly of a heart attack, and with her last breath she asked Maria to make sure that her eleven-week old Boxer pup, which she called JasperJack, went to a good home. Maria called Robbie, who then called Debby.

"You won't believe this story," Debby began. "The puppy is spending the night at Robbie's house. Robbie wants to bring him over to us in the morning just to see him. Rob says he is so cute."

"I don't know. I'm just starting a new life as a retired person," I said, beginning as I usually did now, with the reasons why some idea or suggestion wouldn't work. I still grieved for Rocket. I still ached for him and I still felt so guilty that I was not able to take care of him and not able to save him.

✶ ✶ ✶

The next morning the pup arrived in our kitchen. I knelt down at puppy level. He had that funny pushed-in boxer face, floppy ears, big brown eyes, caramel-colored fur, and white markings on the tip of his nose, each paw, and his chest. He trotted over to me and crawled into my lap. Then he licked my face.

He stayed.

I didn't love him right away. He wasn't my Rocket. But he was adorable and needed constant care.

We wanted to change his name. After trying many new names for him we settled on Koufax, in honor of Sandy Koufax, the great Jewish left-handed pitcher for the former Brooklyn and then L.A. Dodgers. Sandy Koufax is still known for his integrity and dignity because he refused to pitch on Yom Kippur, even though it was the opening game of the World Series. A gentle man with a strong moral compass, he could say no without getting mad as hell.

Our Koufax is well-named.

I decided to begin immediately training him to be a service dog. I took him with me wherever I went so that he would get used to new surroundings and become comfortable with all manner of noises, objects, and people. I sent away for a vest that proclaimed: Service Dog in Training. At first the vest hung loosely around his little puppy frame. He seemed to know that the click of the vest around his stomach meant he had a job to do. He didn't pull or tug or engage in puppy antics when he wore his vest.

I knew a bit about puppy training from my experience with Rocket and from watching Rachel. She gave me a gift of lessons with one of the best trainers in my area.

Once I retired, Koufax and I were together all day. First thing in the morning was Kofi's walk. Without him, I probably would have lingered in bed. But up I'd get, dressing quickly in walking clothes. He would leap out of bed, particularly if he saw me reach for my shoes. Shoes with laces indicated a walk.

"Where shall we go today?" I always asked him. "The field so you can run? No? Do you want to go to the dog park where your brother Rocket bit that guy? I guess you need dogs to play with. Maybe you'll see Petey or HoneyBear. OK, we'll go to the dog park, but remember we have to be out of there by 10:00 a.m. And please don't chase or bark at runners. New rules."

We always talked. I told him what I wanted to do that day or what I was worried about or how I felt in general. Sometimes I'd be unaware that we were in a public place as I continued what was for me an important conversation. When I saw someone, I'd lower my voice and wait until I could resume the conversation with Kofi. I always felt better after I talked to him. I didn't hesitate or reach for what to say or tamp down an emotional edge. I spoke to him in a voice that wasn't strained or self-conscious. My voice sounded more like inner talk that was clearer, smoother, and more articulate than my outward voice often was. He'd look at me and wait. And when I'd signal it was time to walk, he'd leap and wiggle his little stumpy tail. His unfiltered joy rippled through me. That's how I started my day.

After our playtime, I'd have coffee and spend time reading the newspaper. Sometimes we'd go to the Black Sheep Café, Koufax proudly wearing his Service Dog in Training vest. "I'll have a large coffee and a plain bagel, well-toasted, with a schmear of cream cheese. He'll have two pieces of turkey," I'd say, looking at Kofi.

"Sure, JoAnne and Kofi."

Often I was asked, "What kind of service dog is he? Are you training him?" For some time I was agitated by the question. I didn't know what to say but felt pressured to say something. If I said he was my service dog, the next question invariably was, "What do you need him for?"

"He's a companion dog," I'd answer in a clipped voice, trying to discourage more questions.

"What kind of companion? What does he do? Did you train him?"

Now I'd get anxious. *Do I talk about the assault? Do I talk about my injuries?*

"He goes everywhere with me," I'd usually say, hoping to end the conversation. Most people moved on at that point, often murmuring, "I'm sorry."

After I became able to express my anger over the assault, I didn't feel as angry at these genuine attempts to connect. About five years after the assault, I was with Koufax at the Washington National Airport when a young man asked me, "What kind of service dog is he? He's a beautiful dog."

"Thank you for the compliment. I'd rather not say more about the service he provides."

"OK. Thanks. Have a good trip."

✳ ✳ ✳

He grew to be tall and muscled, loyal and well-behaved, accompanying me into restaurants and stores, libraries and public offices. As an emotional support dog, he stayed with me on airplanes, lying at my feet, though he'd rather be sitting in the seat next to me.

His vest cued people not to touch him and not to talk to me. He was a safe barrier when I felt overwhelmed in a crowded space; he helped me to engage in conversation or gave me a way to stop a conversation. He became my constant companion and, with his silly and calming ways, helped me to stay focused on the present moment.

Koufax would accompany me to doctor's visits. I continued to experience visceral reactions to hospital tests and settings—going for a CT scan, the sound of an MRI, getting a blood draw, or the painful test for carpal tunnel syndrome. He required my attention in the moment, making it less likely that I'd wander in my mind to an earlier event.

Once, during an appointment with Dr. Burbrick, she moved to do a simple procedure to test my neurological reactions. As she moved closer to me, Koufax got up from his place and just walked over to me, placing his body between Dr. Burbrick and me. He waited until he sensed that I was fine and, job done, he sauntered back to his spot.

Sometimes I think he was sent by Rocket.

✷ ✷ ✷

More and more is written about how dogs provide invaluable support to people with TBI or post-traumatic stress disorder. I know
that Rocket and Koufax are keys to my survival and recovery. I'm not
investigating what it is about a canine that makes them healers. The
why isn't significant to me. The language of the divine—something
beyond ordinary knowing—has never been a part of the fabric of my
worldview. It wasn't part of my upbringing. I believe, though, that
Rocket gave everything he had in order to help me get through the
first part of my recovery. Then he sent Koufax to be with me for the
next part. To me, they are both divine.

Twenty-Two: I'm Mad As Hell and I'm Not Going to Take It Anymore

I saw the movie *Network* when it was released in 1976. I'm not someone who has lines from movies or books at the ready, but a line from *Network* has always stayed with me. The character that delivers this line is Howard Beale, a longtime TV newsman who has just been fired. His existential rant includes a critique of the summary of the day's violence given on the evening news. He rails against the tally of those killed or violently assaulted that's doled out each day on the evening news. He warns us that this daily diet of violence begins to seem normal, like it's the way life is supposed to be. He then offers a strategy. He tells his listeners to stop what they're doing. Stand up. Open windows and doors. Roll down car windows. Stand on chairs. And yell, "I'M MAD AS HELL AND I'M NOT GOING TO TAKE IT ANYMORE."

Maybe this line has been so important to me because I've never felt entitled to express rage or anger in relation to my own life. I remember after I saw *Network,* I was driving alone and I did it: I opened my car window and shouted, "I'm mad as hell and I'm not going to take it anymore." I felt freer for those few seconds, as though I was part of a group of people, all angry, all determined not to take it anymore, although I couldn't articulate what "it" was at that time in my life.

My mother would get mad, though she didn't encourage her

children to express their anger or any strong feelings. She would yell, maybe throw something, or become very sullen. Her behavior spoke loudly of feelings, but she never offered any words to explain her feelings or the experiences that lay beneath her shouts. She praised *managing*, moving forward, and not dwelling on feelings. She was proud of me for many reasons, including my ability to deal with difficult situations without "making a fuss." When my marriage ended, when Rachel had her accident, when I would face crises at work, she remarked, "You handle things so well."

My father's anger was expressed toward the political world. His knowledge was vast, and his ability to analyze a large swath of information was awe-inspiring. About almost any topic, he could offer a thorough and compelling analysis. He had a wonderful sense of humor and a gift for storytelling. He wasn't pedantic. His positions were clear and, at times, seemed to me unassailable.

About his own private feelings, though, my father was silent. Very silent. I never knew how he felt during the last years of his life, trapped in his body with his mind still alert.

Howard Beale provided a forceful message: *Get mad as hell. Don't take it anymore!* While I loved the message of the movie, I typically expressed my anger using an amalgam of my parents' ways. I was silent and sullen when upset, with most of my anger directed toward political issues. About private concerns, I managed. I'd pick myself up, dust myself off, and start all over again, while trying to be as perky as Fred Astaire dancing.

After the assault, I tried to use the same coping strategies I had used before the assault. My version of dusting myself off was to go back to the gym, go back to work, and tell people that I was *just fine*. What did change, though, was my ability to control and manage my emotions. I could no longer regulate them. I cried; I cried frequently. I yelled. Often there wasn't anything that precipitated an emotional outpouring other than a leaf falling or a loud noise, or my fear that there might be a loud noise. I would snap at Debby for making a sound while chewing gum, or get agitated if Savi had the TV on in his room. I felt angry if someone asked me how I was, or said I looked good, and I was also angry if nobody said anything. The cells in my brain continued to bounce around after the assault, and so did the rest of me.

"Jesus, watch out. There's a car!" I'd say in a high-pitched voice to Debby when we drove anywhere.

"I know, I see it," she'd say, voice tensing.

"Driving makes me so nervous. You need to slow down, watch the oncoming traffic, be careful, we're late," I'd continue. I was suddenly vigilant about all aspects of life.

"What time will you be home for dinner? What do you want to eat? When should we have dinner?" I'd ask her, as if these were the most important questions in my life, requiring clear and immediate answers.

"Savi, turn down the TV. Please turn on your light. I'll help you soon. I can't hear you. I'm resting. I'm so tired."

It wasn't easy to be with me, just as it wasn't easy to *be* me.

✳ ✳ ✳

I wish I could offer an epiphany, describing how I was able to invoke the spirit of Howard Beale, or provide some insight into how I could have gained more emotional understanding sooner in the recovery process. I wish I could point to some sort of intervention that might have helped me act sooner.

Aided by Dr. Jenkins, Debby, and conversations with my brother about our childhood, I became more aware that I was no longer a six-year-old hiding from FBI agents, nor was I lying in an alley anymore. Of course, I had known these truths intellectually for some time, from counseling and from teaching women how to reclaim their voices, give sound to their anger, and understand the legitimacy of their trauma and be visible. But moving away from my oft-told story ("I was a frightened, shy, child and now I live with such trauma") and developing another narrative was difficult.

I began with small steps.

It seems obvious to say that to be more visible, I had to be in places where I could be seen. In my bed, under the covers and watching TV, was not such a place.

I was also learning how to express anger and frustration when I felt these emotions, rather than waiting and letting them fester. For instance, my family doctor was away on vacation when I needed some sort of medical assistance. (After the assault, it seemed as though I was seeing my doctor for an infection or rash or sore throat ever few weeks.)

"I'm here to see the doctor," I politely said to the receptionist.

"Oh, I'm sorry. I'll have to reschedule you."

"That's unacceptable. I'm here. I made the appointment days ago. I need to see a doctor and I won't leave this office until I do."

Within minutes, I was in the doctor's office.

Finally, I had had enough.

I really wasn't mad as hell, but I also wasn't willing to take it anymore. The "it" that was calcifying inside me was about being alone and invisible in the alley. The alley was becoming the representation of so much of my life. My little steps—speaking up, or choosing not to spend time with people who sapped my energy, or initiating a conversation with others—created a softening pause in my story, like a colon: a chance to pause and breathe, but not to come to a conclusive end.

It felt good and different, to be mad and to say something out loud. I did call some people back and apologize for overreacting. My anger often had to do with the mundane: for instance, when someone pushed me while waiting in a line or criticized me for bringing my dog into a public place. "Please do not talk to me in that tone of voice. You don't have to yell, and I don't want your criticism!"

Or letting friends know that I was angry or hurt: "You didn't invite me to that party. Even if I don't go out much, I felt so insulted that you didn't invite me."

✷ ✷ ✷

When my grandson was taking boxing lessons, the trainer tried to coax me into getting in the ring. "It'll be good for you. Give you confidence. You'll be able to protect yourself."

"No thank you."

"Go on," he implored.

"Protect myself? How would YOU protect yourself from someone taller than you who came up behind you with a hammer? How dare you tell me that with a few boxing lessons I could have fended off a man with a hammer! How dare you!"

"I'm sorry," he offered.

I exhaled.

Twenty-Three: Gratitude and
A Party

So many people helped our family get through the countless hurdles that followed the assault. We always expressed our appreciation in person, by writing and through Debby's Caring Bridge posts, but as this particular post notes, we didn't have the time or and energy to say more than "Thank you":

> *Last night we talked about making a list, a long list of all of the people we needed to write specific thank yous to for all of their gifts, food, notes, gift certificates, flowers, services and extreme generosity. It was a long list and since Joannie and I (especially now) are both having severe memory problems, we did not trust ourselves to include everyone. Joannie also said she would be too tired to even make the list, let alone write the cards, and she felt really badly about that. Actually, she fell asleep soon after saying that, right in the middle of our Weeds marathon.*

My retirement provided the opportunity to acknowledge our gratitude more fully. We decided to throw a party, calling it a *gratitude party* rather than a retirement party, and invited everyone who had cooked a meal, offered a ride, or come for a visit. We invited all of my work colleagues and Debby's work colleagues. We invited the many people who extended kindnesses of one sort or another to me, Debby, Rachel, Savian, and Robbie. We invited our neighbors, and our friends and family who lived far away.

During my last months of work, when I wasn't lost in thought or throwing out papers, I focused on the party, which was to be held on September 8, 2012. I wanted the party to be a celebration and something that, in small measure, could express our profound gratitude. I didn't want gifts or potluck food contributions. This, I hoped, would be one glorious evening of talk and laughter, music and fine food: a time to celebrate rather than to reflect on a dreadful event.

I rented the social hall of our local Jewish Community of Amherst facility, a large beautiful room with high ceilings, walls painted in soft yellow hues, and tall windows lining the east and west walls. Gleaming hardwood floors added both a softness and luster to the room.

We set up for about one hundred guests. Round tables were covered with white tablecloths and bouquets of freshly picked dahlias, selected and arranged by Marie, my favorite flower vendor at the Amherst Farmer's Market. Larger bouquets decorated the food and beverage tables.

Food was catered from our local Black Sheep Deli, my home-away-from-home, known by friends as "JoAnne's office." Like so many friends, the Black Sheep brought food to our house during the first year of my recovery and the staff always made me feel safe and taken care of when I was able to go there on my own. Before the party, I sat down with Nick, the owner, to plan the food, which had to comply with kosher standards because it was being held in part of a synagogue. Since we expected one hundred people, I ordered food for one hundred twenty-five. G-d forbid there wouldn't be enough food. Appetizers of crudités, cheese and fruit, crackers and chips with various dips would be available as soon as people arrived. Then eggplant parmesan, pasta and red sauce, a large green salad, sautéed green beans, and baskets of bread would appear. The food portion of the night would be capped with platters heaped with pastries.

I'd always planned to have music at the party. Rachel made a playlist of over one hundred songs that could be played throughout the night. The month before our party, I heard a band play at my nephew's wedding. There was something about the music and the musicians that touched me deeply. After the wedding, I asked them to play at our party. I told them that I wanted music that would make people smile and get up and dance. They didn't disappoint.

Rachel took care of all of the beverage arrangements, deciding what we needed and how much, how to keep certain drinks cold, and how to set up the beverage table. Two cases of red wine. One case of white wine. Three twelve-packs of beer. Six half-liter bottles of Coke and Ginger Ale, and forty-eight bottles of water. Bowls of ice and slices of lemon on the table.

My job was to rest before the party.

The party was our exclamation mark of thanks. We needed so much, and so much was eagerly given. Our plan was to keep the ceremonial portion of the evening very simple. Debby and I would speak. Our friend Jay would read a poem. We wouldn't open the mic for comments or testimonials. Dessert and more dancing would follow our remarks.

By 4:30 p.m. the room was sparkling. Everything was set. I didn't even check the weather—one of my daily rituals—and as a result I missed the tornado warnings being issued for western Massachusetts. I wore a new red dress, short, sleeveless, and rouched in the middle, cream-colored, three-inch patent leather heels, and long red earrings. I was ready to party.

At 5:00 p.m., Arlene and Martha arrived. As they walked through the door, I remembered them waiting for me, literally with open arms, as I came home from the hospital.

As each person arrived, I recalled so vividly what he or she brought or did or said during the three years following the assault. They weren't gloomy memories. My deep appreciation was unblemished by the assault.

Susan and Connie walked in. Susan was one of my drivers. She was a college professor. While together in her car we shared our respective classroom experiences. She talked about her research focusing on the antebellum South. Time in the car passed quickly as we traveled through her childhood, my childhood, and our respective work lives. Connie was one of many who brought us food. With each meal delivery, she attached a beautifully written menu of what each box held and instructions: "Heat the casserole dish for 30 minutes in a 350-degree oven. Let the dish rest for 10 minutes before serving."

The party scene for me was like paging through a coffee table book, beautifully put together with each page containing a distinct image. Each time someone entered, a new picture came into my mind. The golden color of Ange's squash soup; the oblong stainless steel steamer Kristen used to make salmon, topped with her dill sauce and garnished with fresh parsley; Val's heart-shaped meatloaf. Carol's grey Prius charging up my driveway to make sure we were on time for hand therapy. She was the busiest person I knew and the first to sign up to give me rides. As I climbed into her car she would shove aside the papers splayed on the passenger seat, giving me a warm welcome, and then we would start to talk. In my mind I saw her eyes, intense and soft as we wound through local politics and remembrances of our mothers, both deceased.

My logistics organizers, Linda, Andy, and Margaret, arrived. I could see myself sunk into the green chair, its springs hanging on the floor, wearing an old sweatshirt with the sleeves cut to make room for my casts. I remembered them facing me, each with papers in hand and looking as if they were attending an important board meeting. I pictured their eyes, intent on the task and tinged with sadness.

The room quickly filled with laughter, hugs, reunions, and

introductions. The band played upbeat jazz. When the party ended, the musicians said that they could feel the emotion in the room and instinctively played music to match the mood.

More platters of food replaced empty platters. As the tempo of the music went up a notch, Pat started dancing and others quickly joined in. Excluding a brief pause when Debby and I spoke, the dancing didn't stop, the eating didn't stop (there were no leftovers), and the buzz of conversation and rolling pitch of laughter didn't stop.

When I finished greeting and chatting with each person, I sat down. I felt rested and buoyed by the energy in the room. I was glad to sit, though, and just watch. People were engaged with each other and all of the logistics were being taken care of by the Black Sheep staff. I could be in this room, filled with people from so many parts of my life, and still be quiet. I would learn in the years following this party how important it was for me to strike this balance: to be connected and quiet, to feel fully engaged and to safeguard my energy at the same time. It was a moment I continue to savor.

When dinner was over and before dessert was served, Debby and I took a mic from the band and went to the middle of the room to offer our words of appreciation. I stood there and looked around this room. The space was filled with the people who had lifted and bolstered and nurtured our family through a terrible nightmare. I saw my daughter, my stepson, and my grandson sitting together in front of me. Seeing them, I could feel a shift inside of me. I was accustomed to speaking in front of groups. I had written down some remarks to make and then I would sit down. But there was Rachel. This was her experience too. I felt such pride just seeing her, as I always do. And my darling Savi, sitting with some of his friends and in my eyes still so very young. I couldn't look at the three of them without the terrible reality of the assault invading my thoughts and my body. This wasn't only my trauma.

Debby spoke first: "There is so much to say about Joanie . . . not only with her retirement but also about who she is and how she 'made it' to this place, here, today.

"First, I would like to thank all of you for being here and for supporting our family during the last few years. We honestly could not have done it without you. You know, when people would ask me, 'Debby, what do YOU need?' I would never really know what to say. But tonight, I realize I could have said, *you*. All of you here tonight and many who are not here. Thank you.

"Tonight is really a chance to talk and kvell about Joanie. Her grit, determination, courage, and heart. I continue to be in awe of her will to make it here tonight to be with us to celebrate her life as well as her retirement. We are also quite lucky to have our children Rachel and Robbie here, as well as our grandson, Savian."

She smiled at me and handed me the mic. I was starting to feel so self-conscious and aware of being the focus of attention. I took a breath and allowed myself to absorb the celebratory feeling in the room. I smiled back at Debby, looked at our children, and said, "There is no way to truly express my gratitude for all that we have been given in the wake of the assault that changed our lives. This party is a small way to offer something to you. Debby is eloquent and understated about herself, as always. I'm so excited to be able to introduce my family to you: my daughter Rachel, my son Robbie, my grandson Savi, and I think you all know my wife Debby."

I motioned for Rachel, Robbie, and Savi to stand. I knew Rachel would hate being asked to stand but I wanted each of them to be acknowledged. I could feel my head start to tingle and my eyes begin to blur. My sight moved between the words on the paper I held and thoughts bubbling inside of me. I could feel my heart beat a bit faster and I stopped looking at the piece of paper. I was, of course, appreciative for all of the help and love we'd received, but I was not grateful for being nearly beaten to death. *Oh god*, I thought. *How can anyone be grateful for pain and suffering? How can I look at myself, my children, hear my wife, and feel anything but sick that this happened and incredulous that we made it to this day? Please, don't congratulate me. Please no platitudes, just eat and dance.* I exhaled and continued speaking:

"I don't believe that 'things happen for a reason' or that there is a 'gift' embedded in adversity. What happened to me just happened. There was no meaning to it . . ."

Before I continued, I looked to the entrance of the room and saw Big John come in: he seemed to take up the entire opening. I caught his eye and he gazed back as his eyes filled with tears. I felt eased by his presence.

"I do have some ability now to make choices about how I live and what lessons I can derive from this horrendous event. And I know that your provision of food and transportation, cards and calls, messages and stories have been invaluable to my recovery. I am so grateful for the abundance of love and care that you have extended to members of my family. Please eat more. Dance. Enjoy. I love you."

The sounds of children rushing toward the dessert table, chairs being moved, and the comforting babble of chatter and laughter quickly filled the room. I could see the band starting to gather again. I saw an empty table and sat down. At that moment, in that place, surrounded by those people, I felt gloriously content. I wanted this to be a party for everyone, not an event that focused on me. And it was.

Twenty-Four: Another Campaign

Two days after the party, Rachel returned to D.C., Debby went back to work, and Savi went back to school. Kofi and I were now alone in the house. I enjoyed the quiet. I didn't have to calibrate my strength due to work demands and I wasn't preoccupied with plans for the party. There was nothing I had to do except walk with Kofi.

Almost as soon as the band stopped playing, people had started to ask me, "How does it feel to be retired? What will you do now with all your time?"

"Sweep. I love to sweep floors. It's so tangible."

I meant what I said, and I hoped that the odd humor would end the questions I couldn't answer.

Before I retired, I sometimes answered the *what will you do* question by saying, "I want to work on the Obama reelection campaign. I'll have the time." I did want to work on the Obama campaign—and I was continually bombarded by the campaign, not just for money but also with requests to volunteer my time. I intended to respond. I just didn't.

* * *

I was a volunteer during the first Obama campaign, as were most of my friends. I can still remember the grand opening of his local campaign office in late September 2008: when I had arrived, the room was already buzzing. Something big was happening and I was overjoyed to be part of it. When the opening speeches started, the room was filled to capacity. Small children ran around in the back of the room near the refreshment tables, friends were waving and greeting each other, and when the speaker said we were working for the next president of the US and the first black president, I could feel chills run through my body. I joined the throngs in shouting "Obama! Obama!"

We were then told about all of the volunteer help needed and asked to sign up. I volunteered to work in the campaign office, to make telephone calls in the office and at home, and to travel to New Hampshire to campaign and hold signs on election day in New Hampshire. I didn't plan on doing so much, but in that space and with that energy, I even began to think about going to Ohio and Florida to campaign. I was a part of a grand historic happening.

Trips to New Hampshire back then had been great fun. I went several times, with friends and with Debby. Each time we were assigned a list of addresses to canvas in New Hampshire, along with a few directions and an information sheet to fill out and return at the end of the day. We were given packets of campaign material to hand out or to leave on behalf of Obama as well as other democratic candidates running for office in New Hampshire. Before leaving the NH office, we were always briefed on how our work fit into the larger campaign philosophy and the behavior expected of us. Never argue, they told us. Always say "thank you," don't go to a home if you are uncomfortable, don't go to a home if there is a dog that makes you uncomfortable, be respectful of property, don't leave trash, etc.

The driving directions were marginally helpful. Using maps, making a lot of U-turns, and aided by potato chips, chocolate bars, and laughter, we knocked on doors, left wads of material, and effusively thanked people for their time and for going to the polls to vote. On election day, I stood in front of the town hall in Chesterfield, New Hampshire, waving signs, thanking people for voting, and feeling ebullient.

Politics was my family's religion. I was nourished on analyses of what needed to change in order to do what Langston Hughes implored: "Let America be America again . . . It never was America to me." I saw in President Obama's election, and in his reelection, a signal that the United States might be, as Hughes hoped, "the homeland of the free." As a child I felt caught between my craving for hope and inspiration, and my inherited awareness of all that was broken in American society. For me this conflict endured: I needed the buoyancy that accompanies hope in order to feel moored in a world so filled with horrors.

The presidency of Barack Obama was for me deeply personal. I had long felt or sensed what black people knew, in their marrow, about the blood-soaked truths of American history. They knew the violent consequences of irrational loathing based on skin color. They knew that the entrenched antipathy toward people of color, and African Americans in particular, was not just a historical fact but also a contemporary reality.

I knew that, for reasons I could never fathom, people hated Jews, too, and the Jews who had been communists were the worst, the most loathed. The kids in my first-grade class told me all of this. But my parents were kind and generous. And they weren't red and they didn't have horns and I didn't think they killed Jesus. I couldn't understand how these kids could hate my parents. They didn't even know them.

I felt a connection with Barack Obama. He knew that *Justice is a blind goddess, a thing to which we black are wise.* With his intellectual acumen and race consciousness, he could still sing *Hallelujah.* He could still shout words of joy and praise. He knew the political truths and yet still had the audacity to hope. I needed that optimism, and I saw his election as holding the glow of a better day.

* * *

In contrast to that first campaign, though, there was no local office during President Obama's re-election campaign in 2012. A campaign worker located in the Berkshires handled all of western Massachusetts and southern New Hampshire volunteer work via phone calls and email. I continued to be besieged by requests to contribute money and to work on the campaign, and I wanted to help, even though times were different. Mostly, I was different.

By mid-October 2012, I felt it was time to step forward and volunteer. I told myself that it was selfish to stay home and not help out and, as was often the case, I tried to convince myself that I was over the humps and out of the valleys from the assault. I could do my part. I *should* do my part. It was the right thing to do, and the re-election of President Obama was so important to the country and to me. I called the western Massachusetts organizer and offered my services. I didn't want to make phone calls, but I had fond memories of working in New Hampshire in 2008, so I volunteered both Debby and myself. We could do it together and bring Koufax. I signed us up to canvas on two consecutive weekends toward the end of October.

The procedure for canvassing was also different during this campaign. I received an email with the Winchester, New Hampshire address of the campaign office where we were to report and was asked to sign up for a specific block of time. In 2008, we went to Hinsdale, New Hampshire. I was so relieved that we were going to a different location.

We took off on an unusually warm and beautiful fall Saturday morning. Koufax sat eagerly in the back seat. We had the car stocked with snacks, and now that we lived in the world of iPhones and GPS, we had no, or at least fewer, worries about getting lost. Winchester was less than an hour's drive from our home and we chose to drive along the beautiful back roads, rather than on the highway.

After the first bit of excitement and our awe over the beauty of the New England fall, I began to get anxious and to think about the end of the day and coming home. I wanted to be in bed. Anxiety was diluting my enthusiasm, but I didn't dwell on my mood since it was now such a familiar state. I was our navigator, following the GPS on my phone. As we got close, I realized we had actually gone too far.

"We're lost. We went too far!" I bellowed.

"It's fine. We only need to turn around," Debby said in a voice that didn't completely hide her irritation with my ever-present anxiety.

"Just do it," I barked.

A few minutes later we found the address. There weren't a lot of cars parked in front. We walked inside. There were only a few people milling around. We gave our names to someone with a clipboard and we were handed the list of addresses to canvas along with our campaign packets. There were no urns of coffee or boxes of donuts as before.

"Have you done this before?"

"Yes. The last presidential election."

"Great. Come back to this office when you're finished. We will immediately send the data you collect to the main campaign office in Chicago."

We left, packets and lists in hand, but without much gusto. IPhones set. Packets organized. Pencils ready to record what people said, we began our route. The first stop was to let Koufax out of the car. "You can't pee on anyone's property," I told him. "We're here representing President Obama."

We decided to take turns knocking on doors. Debby went first. I talked to Koufax. When she came back, I recorded whether someone was home and if so, if the person was planning to vote for the President, another candidate, or if he or she was undecided.

The second house: my turn. I went to the door and began to feel increasingly uneasy. It somehow felt too familiar. No one was home. I left the material and ran to the car.

"*You* need to go the houses. It triggers me too much. I'll keep the logs and take care of Koufax." As always, Debby complied with my demands, in part because of her good nature and in part because I was so volatile.

We continued for another four or five or six houses. I don't remember now how many houses we went to before everything was clearly recognizable. It wasn't just the process that was familiar, but I could now definitely recall each house. I knew where the gates were. I could remember what the people looked like and what they would probably say. I recalled their dogs, their gardens, and the color of the curtains in their windows.

Something's not right, I thought. *I feel like I'm in a Stephen King movie. Not just familiar, but like I've been* exactly *here. In front of this house. Last year they had red geraniums in that planter box. This year the geraniums are that deep peach color. The door is on the side of the house and the woman who'll answer the door is an avid Obama supporter.*

My recollection was so vivid, but why? Was I seeing a memory or was I seeing what was before me? Had I slipped back to 2008?

"You're anxious," Debby offered. "Things just seem familiar. We're on a typical rural New Hampshire road. Let's just go to the next house."

The next address was only a short distance away. Debby turned left and drove up a rather steep driveway. She parked on the level landing. Beautiful flagstone steps led to the front door. Multi-colored begonias in window boxes still bloomed, framing the white lace curtains hanging in the front windows. A lovely New England image. A dog inside of the house barked. Debby rang the doorbell but no one answered. She stuck the material inside the screen door and was walking toward the car when a man came out of the side door and stood on the landing.

"I'm a libertarian," he said. "Tell whoever sent you that I don't want any more calls or material. Just stay away. I didn't vote for Obama last time and I won't this time or any time."

He was shouting. His hand was clenched in a fist and he was waving his arm in the air like an exclamation mark, with added punctuation given from his barking dog. Because he was standing on a porch and we were parked downhill from him, he seemed bigger and more menacing. The strength of his fury frightened me. He turned and went back inside. The dog continued to bark.

It was precisely the same scenario as four years before. Same house. Same dog. Same angry man. Same message.

Debby quickly got in the car.

"You're right. Same man. Same house. Let's go," she said.

We were stunned. We had started at a different campaign location but now we were somehow on the exact same canvassing route that we'd been assigned four years ago. I reached into the glove compartment and pulled out a map of New Hampshire. I saw that in 2008, we began the route in Hindsdale, NH and drove north, and this time we'd started in Winchester and had driven south. But we were on the same road and going to the same houses.

I froze. I was tumbling back in time. As was often the case during moments when I felt frozen, I was unable to move or think. I went back to the moments in the alley; I could feel the sensations in my body as I entered the void. My head began to tingle and my heart beat faster. I could feel myself getting flushed. I was terrified and confused.

Debby suggested that we return to the campaign headquarters, hand in what we had collected, and go home. She brought all of the papers we had into the campaign office. I stayed in the car, this time not even talking to Kofi. What had seemed like a quaint New Hampshire town now felt like the scene of a scary movie. There were no people walking on the street or children playing outside. The trees were bare and some of the plants in window boxes were wilting. I began to feel claustrophobic. I was reminded of the movie *The Truman Show*, where the character played by Jim Carrey lives in a community that at first seems perfect: wholesome, clean, and safe. At the denouement of the movie he discovers that he is actually living on a movie set and what he thought was just the horizon is really the edge of the canvas tent that encircles the "town." I didn't remember anything else about the movie, but the horrible feeling remained vivid, as the main character realizes something that had once seemed ideal has become a nightmare.

My daily reality was already skewed. Nearly four years after the assault, I still feared going into familiar settings, avoided conversations with people I loved, and experienced my body reacting seemingly on its own to stimuli. I still jumped or yelped at various sights and sounds. And now here I was, in this surreal experience, reenacting scenes from the first Obama presidential campaign but without the elation I'd felt in 2008. Also, my own ennui was seemingly matched by a broader political lassitude. The *Yes We Can* momentum had hit congressional gridlock and political compromise. Electing the first African American president released grand expectations of what he could and should achieve in four years, as well as the conscious and unconscious racism that permeates United States culture. The re-election campaign had a different energy.

We drove to another town and stopped at a restaurant for lunch. We were both shaken by the strangeness of the day and realized we were more eager to get home than we were to be sitting down for lunch. I took Kofi on a short walk, Debby got our sandwiches to go, and we took the quickest, non-scenic road home.

After a few days I called the contact person and told her that I couldn't do any more volunteer work and I told her why. She thanked me profusely and wished me well.

✶ ✶ ✶

I may have underestimated the reactions I would experience by taking part in President Obama's re-election campaign, but I could not stem the flood of emotions that poured out as the second inauguration approached. My mind was stuck on instant replay and I saw the days preceding January 16, 2009, with cinematic clarity.

Scenes replayed and replayed. If I forgot a detail, I would "rewind" to start again and see each moment *before*. The new snow pants had pockets. Were they on the side or back pockets? Think again. Was it a glazed or chocolate-covered donut I had at the airport before flying to D.C.? What did I see in the airport gift shop that I thought of getting before my flight home? Was I wearing a red or black neck warmer on the walk to Rachel's house? I was lodged in the *post* part of PTSD, reviewing, reliving, and revisiting the trauma. The inauguration of President Obama had had so much meaning for me, and my attempt to attend his first inauguration had been filled with such jubilation. Now, as the second inauguration approached, I was propelled back to that moment in which my body and my life were rearranged. The assault was my personal horror. And feeling hope, not for the world but for me, was a Sisyphean task.

✳ ✳ ✳

I was elated, of course, when he was re-elected. It felt like an achievement even greater than the first election. He was no longer attempting to be the first black president. He was President, a black president, with flaws on display. People on all sides of every issue expressed disappointment with what he didn't do or didn't do sufficiently or shouldn't have done at all during his first term. And yet he won.

Debby and I decided to avoid the media blitz of his second inauguration day. In the morning we went to the gym and then out to breakfast. We took Kofi on a long walk and then went to a movie to get lost in the magic created by the big screen. By the end of the day,

I could listen to clips of the inaugural speech and in the evening take pleasure in seeing Michelle's gown.

Rachel, on the other hand, could not escape the inaugural activities. Streets in her neighborhood were closed; roads coming into D.C. were closed. The sidewalks near her home were crowded with people delighted to be heading for the National Mall and all the festivities. She'd spent President Obama's first inauguration in George Washington University Hospital agonizing over my condition and his second inauguration trying just to get through the day.

We were all relieved when the actual inauguration was over.

Twenty-Five: And On and On and On

Toward the end of 2012, and after the re-election of President Obama, I was home one day, doing ordinary things. I needed to use the bathroom and, seconds later, found myself in our basement, where there is no bathroom, loosening the snap on my jeans.

It happened that I had an appointment soon after this incident with Dr. Burbrick, my neurologist, in Boston. I told her about the episode in the basement. She was very concerned and thought that perhaps I'd had a temporal-lobe seizure. While the major blows of the assault were to my frontal lobe, once a brain experiences a powerful impact, the billions of cells reverberate for a long time, causing injury to various locations in the brain. *It goes on and on.* She was most concerned about the moments of disorientation and loss of time. Losing time is different from going to the refrigerator and forgetting why; it is not knowing how you got to the refrigerator. She suggested I go through a forty-eight-hour EEG.

Another schlep to another hospital. The directions sent in advance said, "Don't wear any clothing that has to go over your head. Wear pants that are easy to take on and off." We arrived on time, although it was a two-hour drive to the hospital. When we got to the room noted in the directions, no one was around. I had a Twilight Zone feeling. Rooms with white walls, hospital beds, and computerized equipment, but no people. And then someone entered:

"Ms. Jones? Follow me please." I followed her to yet another white room with a white hospital bed.

"Have you ever had an EEG?"

"Many."

"OK. This is similar except it stays on your head for forty-eight hours. I'll attach one part of the electrode to your head and the other end to a battery pack that you'll need to keep on the whole time. Your brain rhythms will be recorded. I'll give you extra batteries just in case."

"How do they stay on my head?'

"With glue."

* * *

I was so proficient now at finding that Zen place. I put myself into the patient role immediately. Followed instructions. Thanked her for her efforts. Told her everything was fine.

I wore a hooded sweatshirt with a zippered closure, as instructed, and when we left the hospital I put the hood over my head, now bulging with glued-on electrodes. We drove home mostly in silence; it wasn't just because of another procedure, but also the suggestion that I could have more brain damage. Lost time. Was I now moving into a new stage, where I would be unaware of seconds or minutes? Find myself someplace I didn't intend to go?

I stayed home for forty-eight hours. I looked odd and I didn't want to answer any questions about why my head was covered with electrodes or what I was carrying in the fanny pack. We returned two days later. Removing the electrodes took only fifteen minutes.

The EEG showed no brain anomalies, but it was another event. Another thing to worry about.

Twenty-Six: The Pull to Write

I continued to feel a tug to write after my writing escape with Rocket, in spite of my various medical and emotional ups and downs. In my head, I started outlining sections of a book. Then I revised the sections. Sometimes I would write these thoughts down in a folder I called Odds and Ends. I continued to clip articles and do computer searches for memoirs and first-person accounts of TBI and PTSD. As the urge to write gained momentum, in early 2013 I decided to clean the room upstairs that I referred to as my office. I dusted, mopped, polished, threw papers away, and created a space that would be exclusively for this writing project. Then I printed some hard copies of what I'd already written, including the Odds and Ends, and placed them in a green folder. I decided to use green folders for everything connected with this book. I associated red with alarm, or red pen on student papers. Blue seemed too cool and dispassionate. Green, the color of earth and growth, seemed to hold the best image. When I found articles I thought were pertinent to my story, they went into a green folder. Clipped newspaper articles about trauma, violence, and TBI—green folder. Internet searches for blogs about trauma, violence, and TBI—green folder.

I found it difficult to develop a daily schedule for writing. There was always a floor to sweep, laundry to fold, or a doctor's appointment to keep. Spring required putting flowers in pots on the deck and summer demanded that I go outside just because it was warm. When I did write, I kept returning to the beginning because that was the habit I'd formed, and because I really didn't know what to write after telling the story of the assault and its immediate aftermath.

* * *

In January 2014 I decided to return to Sanibel Island. Bring Koufax. Get disciplined about writing.

Debby drove us to Florida and returned to drive us back home, a mitzvah of enormous proportions. I only told friends and family that I was going to Florida to get away from the New England winter. I didn't announce that I was writing a book because that seemed too pretentious, too big, too real. I wasn't ready to think of myself seriously as a writer.

I brought the green folders and books on trauma and traumatic brain injury. I had ample space to spread out and immediately organized a writing area for myself. Pens and pencils, sticky notes, and paper clips carefully placed in a basket. Green files stacked on one side of the dining room table, aka work desk. Books stacked next to the green file folders arranged by size. I am not typically an über-organized person, but I needed to construct an environment that encouraged and invited writing. "Yah, this looks good," I thought. The workspace conveyed that I was engaged in an important project. Koufax lay down wherever he wanted to, with his head usually resting on a pillow.

I was able to develop and stay with a writing schedule. After a walk and breakfast, and a bit of sweeping, I would go immediately to the dining room table for about three hours. I made an outline of what I wanted to include in the book and how I thought the book should be organized, with notes about specific stories to include. Some days the time was mostly spent researching information. Other days I'd write, finally moving beyond the assault and immediate surgeries and medical issues.

I didn't notice the passage of time until I looked up at the clock. My story enveloped me, not only with pain, but also with curiosity to find out where I would be guided by my own creativity. I didn't think about the craft of writing; I didn't think about where to put semicolons or about creating clear transitions between sections. I jumped between tenses. This time, the scribe was my imagination, not a specific picture circling around and around. At times, what I produced was more like a stream of consciousness: thoughts and feelings pouring out in a seemingly random order. Fatigue was my signal to stop when words became harder to find or the page began to blur.

Going to the beach was my payoff for writing. I brought a supply of books for pleasure reading but found that I mostly turned to memoirs about TBI or violence, books about stages of trauma and signs of TBI. I was looking for ideas about how TBI memoirs were structured and I wanted to know how "real" writers constructed their stories. I was looking for templates to help with my own writing. As I walked with Koufax, I thought of new ideas to include or found wording that had eluded me while sitting at the dining room table. I was fully engaged, involved, and focused. By the end of the month I was committed to completing the book.

Writing found a fertile place inside of me, a place that was not broken or damaged: a place that, when fed by thoughts and words, grew and blossomed. Writing scratched an itch I didn't realize I had. It fed a hunger that lay dormant under the layers of fatigue and fear I'd acquired since the assault.

* * *

I now see writing this book as an act of courage. When I started, I didn't understand that writing had anything in common with finding the strength to look in a mirror, to be bathed by an indifferent stranger, or to endure endless pain. Through writing, I slowly began to realize that to tell my story, I had to uncover and reveal a great deal of myself. I had to learn to tolerate discomfort and uncertainty. I had to just let things be, and I had to engage and move forward without knowing what the outcome would be.

Trauma and TBI gave me ample reasons to stop writing whenever I chose: *It's so difficult to concentrate. I simply don't have the energy for a major project right now. It's too triggering. I can't go back into that experience. I'm too tired. My hands hurt.* Everyone would understand if I decided to stop writing or take more time or leave out sensitive incidents. People would be sympathetic and tell me how courageous I was even to attempt to write about the assault. "I can't believe you're able to write about the accident . . . er, what happened. It must be so very painful," were comments I often heard.

I didn't want sympathy or a way out, but I was flooded with self-doubt. Could I really stay with this? What did I have to say that would be of significant value to anyone other than my family and friends? What if I couldn't manage my feelings? Would what I wrote hurt someone? How would I manage criticism? Questions produced more questions.

✳ ✳ ✳

Just as I couldn't do yoga without an instructor, I realized that to be serious about writing meant I needed practical, ongoing guidance. To keep plugging along on my own meant a start-and-stop pace, with starting invariably succumbing to stopping.

I began to look for writing workshops and classes. I didn't restrict myself by geography. I imagined a month-long writing retreat or programs of a similar ilk. There were many. I needed direction as well as the space to write and a community to write with. Over the next weeks I searched on Google, looking for writing opportunities. I found this:

The Manuscript Series is a ten-month program for writers with prose manuscripts in progress that call for critical response and new writing. Writers can be working on novels, short story collections, memoirs, or essay collections. This group will provide the structure, support, inspiration, and critical feedback to help writers complete a book-length manuscript.

I thought this had been written just for me. Plus, the workshop was located close to my home. It had all the pieces I was looking for.

To apply was to take a step outside of my cocoon. It meant making myself vulnerable and visible. What if I wasn't accepted? What if I didn't fit into the group? What if it was too much? I'd have to leave my house and interact with people I didn't know. I knew that many of my feelings were not unusual. Fears about competence and acceptance are not exclusive to people who have been traumatized.

There was another layer of trepidation, one I didn't share with anyone. I knew my story was powerful and dramatic. *Bludgeoned with a hammer and lived to tell the tale.* But I wanted to write mostly about what happened *after* the assault. I wanted to help people who have had similar experiences. I was a helper and a teacher, so I wanted to help and teach. Otherwise, why write at all? Beyond the altruism was the fear that my story was really a sham. Sure, it was a horrible thing, but in truth I barely remembered it. I remembered what I wrote about the moment of the assault, but I didn't think that was the same as walking around with a memory of more significant traumas, such as war or living with violence on a daily basis. Sure, there were painful times while I was in the hospital, after hand surgery and after the seizure, but now I felt fine. *I'm fine. I've managed just fine. What do I really have to write about? What do I say after the line, "I won't let the assault define me?" What do I write about after I acknowledge the*

importance of the outpouring from family, friends, and community? I
mean, isn't that sufficient?

These thoughts swirled around, perched in the background as I talked about applying for the Manuscript Series and my desire to write a book. Both Doctors El Chemali and Jenkins enthusiastically encouraged me to apply. I didn't tell them about my belief that my writing would be fraudulent. The internal dialogue of doubt and recrimination remained lodged in my mind, even after I was accepted and started to anticipate the first weekend of meeting the group members and receiving feedback about my writing. The yammering inside of me didn't just evaporate, but it became weaker as the comments from the group and facilitator got louder.

The structure of the Manuscript Series involved eight 2-day group intensives, spread over ten months. Meetings were held Friday evening and all day Saturday. Each participant was expected to read the submissions of all group members prior to the weekend workshops. We would then meet and focus for about an hour on the work submitted by each author, beginning always with positive comments about what was working, then comments or questions about the narrative, and ending with each commenter reading a portion of the narrative that was particularly impactful. Then a break for food, beverages, chatter, and laughing. Between each of these weekend sessions, we were expected to produce about forty-five pages of new writing.

The structure was perfect for me. It was clear and demanding. I knew what was expected. The atmosphere in the group set by the facilitator, Dori Ostermiller, helped me to concentrate on writing and put worries about editing aside—to quell the internal editor that questioned the quality of the writing.

With the aid of other readers, I saw how my initial writing was like reading Cliffs Notes: complexity condensed into brief paragraphs. In my first draft about the seizure, for instance, I simply said that I'd suffered a seizure and then returned to work a few days later. I was embarrassed to write about waking up in my own excrement and admitting to the terrible shame and humiliation I felt. There were ways in which this writing was similar to the first time Big John told his story in my class: it was rushed, with no transitions between parts and incidents that bounced from one time period to another, and he was emotionally spent when he finished.

I could write for long stretches at a time. Whether I was writing at home, in Florida, or the Amherst College Library, I could block out everything around me and enter the world of words and ideas. I would search for the right word to describe what I was thinking. As is often the case with writing, more ideas stayed in my head than hit the page. After writing several pages or spending an hour on a particular incident, I would start to feel embarrassed. It was that old feeling of taking up too much space, being too visible, saying too much. Who was I to take up so much of people's time with all these pages? *It's enough already*, I'd say to myself, dredging up one of my mother's frequent comments to my brother and me during our sibling confrontations. *"Enough already!"* she'd bellow, and we knew it was past time to stop whatever we were doing.

This wasn't journal writing, nor was I writing in isolation. Whatever conversations I had with myself, there were six other readers with their own thoughts and comments about what I'd written. During our weekend intensives, their comments were offered with detailed reference to the narrative, with the intention of helping to make the piece stronger, and with the insight that accompanies thoughtful analysis. The first time someone read my words about the assault and referred to me not by my name but as *the narrator*, I felt chills. I heard my *story* and its intensity from the perspective of a reader or listener.

Writing exposed me. I had learned to be silent and to fear visibility as a very young child. I understood that the consequences of speaking and being seen were dire. I had only to recall the Rosenbergs to have that lesson reinforced. I had learned to loathe being visible as a Jewish girl and woman. I knew that Jews were feared and Jewish woman were not pretty. Years of shame and silence had soldered these feelings into me. As a professional educator, I became proficient at using my childhood experiences as examples of "isms" and in the analysis of social systems and social stigma. But the welding inside of me held.

The assault had bombarded every part of me. Theories, beliefs, expectations, competencies, self-perception, feelings—all in disarray. During the time I was desperately seeking explanations for TBI and PTSD, a wonderful psychologist told me that traumatic brain injury was like a filing cabinet that gets thrown in the air. When it lands, some things drop into familiar places and some things stay rearranged or lost. Writing was like cleaning out my office, with the added challenge of TBI. I had to go through files, throw some out, stop worrying about the ones that were missing, and find a new way to arrange what was important and what no longer mattered.

I wanted to be silent and not talk to anyone, and I also wanted to shout and scream about what had happened to me. I wanted to be invisible and was enraged when people didn't *see* me as my current, rearranged self. It was easy enough to write about my rage in relation to racism, violence, and the criminal justice system. But uncovering and then exposing my more personal feelings was more difficult. It was painful to write about the roots of wanting to be invisible, the shame that I spent a lifetime trying to keep hidden from almost everyone, and the powerful sanctions against talking about family that were wedged deep inside of me. As I continued to write about the assault, I became increasingly aware of what remained buried.

✱ ✱ ✱

I remember lying in bed at GW Hospital feeling reassured and comforted by my own stoic, tolerant demeanor. I was minimally in touch with what was going on around me, but at least I was handling this misery appropriately. Just like my father would. I was a lot like my father in the way I responded to difficult times—patient and stoic. I endured what needed to be endured without voicing distress, let alone anger. It was the right thing to do because it was what he had done.

I knew if he asked for help, he would only ask once. In my family, we don't ask. And we never ask a second time. We manage. We remain stoic. We move forward the best we can. With two broken hands and a fractured skull, I didn't want to ask for help. Under what circumstances *would I ever ask?*

Writing has been my miner's light, making visible words and pictures in my head and arranging them like a Rorschach test. Listening to the patterns other readers see helps me to see and feel the assault from different perspectives. Untangling the fragments and stories of my life was a crucial step in learning how to live with the extreme violence I experienced and all of its ramifications.

I'm often asked, "Is the writing painful? Does it bring up difficult memories? Is it hard to write this? Is it therapeutic?"

Yes.

Yes, there were painful parts, times of confusion and disorganization, long periods where words arrived like precious gems, rare and infrequent, and times when the words flowed in an inchoate stream. The chaos of writing was painful.

Yes, it's hard. Not just because I'm telling the story of a heinous assault. The whole voyage of writing brings up all kinds of painful memories and experiences. Writing has asked me to push the boundaries of exposure and vulnerability. Writing demands that I not stay invisible, that I keep the assault in my face and find the strength to make others stare at it as well. Writing demands authenticity, telling the truth about what I've lost, how I've cloaked myself in the protective identity of victim, and how my views of justice and oppression have been altered.

Yes, it's therapeutic. Not only because I tell and reveal this story, but also in the deep satisfaction of seeing what happened to me in many contexts and at many levels.

Writing, an important character in my story, implores me to find the courage to move forward and the courage to be patient when I can't move at all.

Twenty-Seven: A Club I Don't Want to Be a Member Of

After I began to write in earnest, Debby and I were invited to an open house party. I rarely went to gatherings and typically felt anxious beforehand. The questions. The comments. The noise. I continued to feel most comfortable at home and now I wanted to use my energy to write.

We walked in, greeted our hosts, and began the ritual of saying hello to friends and offering perfunctory glad-to-meet-you to others. I saw a friend who, like me, had recently retired from an academic job. I went toward her, finding it easier to engage in conversation with one person rather than to move around the room, wine glass in hand, having cordial exchanges with many people. Just as we were beginning our conversation, her companion George walked over. "You must try the chicken salad, it's delicious," he interrupted. I was immediately angry. *Just like a man*, I thought. *Has to take over the conversation.*

"What are you doing now?" my friend asked, not responding to the chicken salad comment.

"I'm writing a book," I declared loudly, embarrassed by the intensity of my response.

"Oh, what are you writing about?" she asked with genuine curiosity.

"The assault. I'm writing about the assault," I replied, trying to modulate my voice.

Then the man started talking about something. I don't recall what. My agitation revved up again. "I'm writing about being beaten with a hammer," I proclaimed defiantly, determined not to be pushed aside by another man.

His expression changed immediately. He didn't have the look that says *"How shocking!"* or *"How can I possibly respond?"* His facial muscles softened, his jaw relaxed, and his shoulders lowered. He moved a step toward me but said nothing for a few seconds. And then, in almost a whisper, "My father was killed by a man with a hammer."

"Oh no. I'm so sorry for bringing this up. I'm so sorry," I said, stunned by his comment and embarrassed by my ire. We talked quietly and intensely. He spoke in the rushed cadence that I often do when telling someone about my assault. He said that his father owned a business and was at work after closing time, that he was a hard worker, and everyone knew that he carried money in a belt around his waist.

"The guy was after money and must have seen the hammer, grabbed it and hit my father to take the money," he said. "I think I know who the guy is, but the police didn't have enough information to charge him."

George was now close to eighty years old. His father had been killed fifteen years earlier. I just listened, repeating how sorry I was that this had happened in his life. When he finished his story, he looked at me intently. "Can I hug you?" he asked.

* * *

I am a member, albeit involuntary, of a strange club, Victims of Violence, and its subset, Victims of Hammer Assaults and Their Families. There is something the members know, but it is an understanding without descriptive language. When George told me about his father, I returned to the abyss, the place with no light, no time, no safety, and no boundaries. I could feel George's isolation as he walked through his days holding an experience impossible to share—a *hammer*, an ordinary tool, a word with a variety of meanings and a common metaphor. For us it now meant terror and sorrow.

I don't know how long we talked. I think it was a long time. We had arrived at the party around 4:00 p.m. and it was now dark outside. From my periphery, I noticed other people at the party moving around, getting food and more to drink. People were beginning to leave. I made a move toward the food table and then turned and hugged George again.

The members of my club increase exponentially. We don't know each other. Our friends and neighbors and politicians decry the violence we've experienced and live with; they forget and move on—or they remember, and still move on.

✶ ✶ ✶

There was a shooting today. It happened in Colorado or Kansas, Washington or Maine. A young man went into a place where ordinary people were doing the most ordinary of things. Two girls were giggling in the school cafeteria. A young boy just learning how to write his name. A woman buying a new dress for her niece's wedding. A retired fireman reaching into a bag of popcorn waiting for the movie to start. The shooter went to a school, a shopping mall, a movie theater, a museum, or a church. He stood in a parking lot or at a gas station. He killed two or eight or twenty people and then he killed himself. He was heavily armed. Reports say that he was mentally ill or depressed; he was angry because he was being bullied or because his parents were getting a divorce. He was struggling in school or he was very bright. He played video games or listened to hard rock music. Police are trying to find a motive for the killings. His parents are horrified.

In another community, a four-year-old child found a gun. He picked it up and accidently shot his brother or sister, cousin or friend. His parents don't know how he found this gun.

In a ghetto, barrio, hood, or housing project, a mother hears a knock at the door. She opens it, heart racing. She sees a man, old already at thirty-two. She recognizes him as the founder of an organization trying to stop the violence in their community. He says, "I'm sorry." Her child had gone to the corner store for milk or crossed the street and was caught in gunfire or had an argument on the schoolyard. He holds her heaving, sobbing body in his arms. When he leaves, he goes to a place to be alone and then he weeps. He weeps for the mother who has outlived her child, he weeps for the child who died before he had a chance to live, and he weeps for himself, enduring another unbearable heartbreak.

I follow each story. I hope the person who died did not suffer in the last seconds of life, in the vortex of the abyss. I hope she wasn't paralyzed with fear. I hope he saw something soft and soothing in his mind's eye.

I hope the survivors find solace in their faith or their friends or their activism, or in quiet moments alone with their grief. I hope there is support for them when they can't stop weeping or worry that they can't weep at all. Support when they are so very tired and unable to focus. Support when they cannot find pleasure in things or people that once held such joy. I hope those who were spared a fatal bullet find a way to come to terms with feeling both guilty and relieved that they are alive.

All now join our invisible club made up of the legions of us whose lives are shadowed by violence.

Twenty-Eight: Crazy Human
with Hope

I have tinnitus now. It just appeared about a year or so after the assault, like a bruise when you don't recall bumping into anything. I first noticed it during the warm summer months of 2010. We had our bedroom windows open. "Do you hear those birds? They are making such a racket," I said to Debby, annoyed with the nonstop buzzing sounds I heard. I imagined a huge flock of birds perched on the branches of the red maple in front our house. *What else other than birds would make that racket?* I thought.

"No," she said absentmindedly.

"You don't hear all that loud noise outside the window?

"*NO.*"

I got up to close the windows and assert my point about this noise invasion by blocking the din with shut windows. But the sounds continued and continued. I realized with horror that the sound was in me, not encroaching from the outside. I didn't know at that moment that the sounds would be permanent residents in my head.

More doctors, more tests, and a diagnosis of tinnitus. Tinnitus is described as a ringing in the ear or ears. I don't hear ringing, as in a bell. I hear *ZZZZZZZZzzzzzzzz*, as in the sound that can be heard when standing under a live electric line. Hissing. *Hisssszzzssing.*

Now I know that tinnitus isn't really a sound; rather it reflects electric impulses gone astray as nerves from the auditory system enter the temporal lobe. Its etiology is not fully known.

The first doctor I saw attributed the tinnitus to genetics. He said that the patterns he saw in the data from a hearing test typically meant the cause was genetic.

"Does anyone else in your family have tinnitus or use a hearing aid?"

"My brother, I think. My mother died recently. She didn't hear well at all during her later years. She always said that if there was something worth hearing, she'd *hear it!*" I said, trying with a humorous story to distance myself from another health intrusion in my life.

The doctor didn't smile.

"Well, your mother probably should have used a hearing aid when she was your age."

"Will a hearing aid take away the noise?"

"No. It will enhance your hearing."

I didn't ask if that meant that the hissing would be HISSING. Would make the constant noise LOUDER.

Tinnitus, I've read, can also be caused by ear cell damage, age-related hearing loss, exposure to loud sounds like gun blasts, ear wax blockage, ear bone changes, a variety of illnesses, or head injury.

I asked the ear specialist, "Why did it start after the assault?"

"I don't know for sure," he said. I had told him all about the assault and the hammer. The story seems to gush out when I am in a doctor's office.

Whatever the cause, once it arrives, tinnitus stays forever. The etiology matters less to me now. The simple truth is that I have tinnitus and it's not going anywhere. I have to live with it or, more accurately, I have to keep finding ways to live with some measure of equanimity in my noisy world. Whatever route tinnitus took to enter my life, it is now symbiotically linked to the sequalae of TBI and PTSD in the assault's aftermath.

Tinnitus often serves as the town crier for its hosts. The ever-present *hissssing* keeps the changes in my life in the forefront of my awareness:

> *Hey, hypervigilance, don't let down your guard. You're not really thinking of going to that party with so many people? If you go to that workshop you might get too tired and then you'll be sorry. Watch out, there's a car! Wait longer before you cross the street. Wait longer before you enter traffic. Just wait.*
>
> *Don't make eye contact as you walk down the street, look straight ahead. Just look at Kofi. Let them know you have protection. You made a wrong turn, AGAIN! Go home, take a nap, ssssSSSSsSsSsS . . . turn on the TV. Do something to block the sounds, you're not following the conversation! Say something innocuous, don't embarrass yourself. Look what that crazy fucker with the hammer has done to your life.*
>
> *Please stop the noise. PLEASE stop the noise. PLEASE STOP THE NOISE.*

There are times when the noise is so loud I can't bear it. I can't escape it. I can't find a Zen place. I can't practice breathing exercises. The noise covers everything, infiltrates all parts of me and makes it impossible to enjoy anything. Silence can make it worse, only intensifying the noise. Sometimes what helps is silence. Other noises can block out the *hisssssssing* but can also cause so much stimulation that my head begins to throb and I feel like I am the exposed part of an electrical cord. No one else hears what I hear or even knows that there is something happening inside me. It is excruciating.

There are, however, times when I can luxuriate in unconscious bliss and simply reside in the moment. Like in the writing group, when everyone is focused on an intense piece of writing, and a very funny line is read or interjected into the conversation and the room erupts in that special kind of laughter that massages the soul. I'm just there in that room, with those people, in that moment sailing on the breath of laughter. In that moment, the only sound I hear is the laughter in me and around me. Or when Debby and I are binging on a TV series, watching one show after another as we merge our own lives into our forty-two-inch flat-screen TV that used to stand near the wall of our bedroom but is now closer to the bed to accommodate our aging eyes. In addition to the hundreds of channels we get through cable, our TV is Smart, capable of streaming even more television shows and movies into our home at any given time. Through TV, I travel to England during World War II with *Foyle's War*, or work in the advertising industry with *Mad Men*.

When I'm writing, the only sounds I hear are my fingers touching the computer keyboard. I get lost in the story I'm telling and the art of writing. I am unaware of any internal noise. I'm unaware of my noise when I'm binging on a TV show, watching Kofi prance into the surf, or laughing with Debby.

More often than not, I hear the sound; it's back there, buzzing, *zzzzzing*, loud and then soft, competing for my attention and then fading into the background. I am learning simultaneously to be aware of the constant noise and to focus on something else. I am learning how to co-exist with the intrusions into my interior being and continue with the business of living. So I hear the sounds in my head, I see my hands; I feel the ridges in my scalp and counsel the person who washes my hair at the beauty salon not to be alarmed when her fingers run across these indentations. I jump when I hear a loud sound. I take naps and often decline invitations to evening events. I ask the waiter to turn down the sound in a restaurant and prefer not to sit with my back facing the entrance. And I go on with my life.

Twenty-nine: Taking Flight

I was on an airplane recently flying from California back to the East Coast. I had seat 40C, the aisle seat on the last row of the plane, the one that abuts the restrooms available for all passengers flying economy. The galley was about five or six feet beyond row forty. After the food and beverage service was over, there was less commotion in the tail section of the plane. Passengers were more settled, watching a movie or sleeping or being occupied by something that helped to while away the time before landing. I was reading a magazine. It was one of the moments when I was completely focused on what I was reading and oblivious to the movements or sounds around me. A rare moment indeed.

Then I felt something hit my head. I gasped and reflexively put my arms over my head and kept them there.

I heard the flight attendant say, "I'm so sorry. Are you okay?" The overhead bin above me was ajar and she was trying to move luggage to reduce the prospect of a passenger getting hurt. A piece of luggage had fallen and hit my head. "Can I bring you some ice? Do you want anything?"

"Ice would be good," I said in a barely audible voice, arms still wrapped around my head.

As soon as she left to get the ice, I started to cry. I wasn't hurt and I wasn't in pain, but I was shaken. She returned with ice wrapped in a plastic bag and covered with a towel. I told her I had a head injury.

"Were you in an accident?"

Man. Hammer. Skull fracture. Broken hands . . . I offered a short version of the most dramatic parts.

She inhaled audibly. "Please let me know if I can do anything for you."

I kept the ice on my head for about half an hour. During that time, I was able to calm down, get my breathing back to normal, realize that I wasn't hurt, and remind myself that I was on a plane and not in an alley.

I stood up and went to the galley to return the ice.

"I think I've ruined your day," I said to Rene, the flight attendant. She smiled, looking a bit more relaxed. Her colleague was sitting on the jump seat flipping through the pages of a magazine.

"We're flight attendants," Rene said, "so we're always curious and ask a lot of questions. Can you tell us what happened?"

I told the whole story.

"Oh my," Rene sighed. "I'm so sorry that happened to you. We hear and see so much."

"Did you read about that man who served twelve years in jail for a crime he didn't commit? He was on my flight last week. I didn't know what to do except hug him. And I watch all of those crime shows."

Then they both told me stories about the rapes and assaults faced by attendants during overnight stops.

"People know the hotels used by flight crews. It's really scary."

We looked at each other. Thirty-five thousand feet in the sky flying over someplace. I felt as though I were talking to friends, sharing stories—some personal, some not as directly personal—all about the hazards of maneuvering through our world with all its horrors, as fellow travelers.

Then the conversation turned to TV programs.

"*Law and Order* is my favorite program," Rene mused. "My brother tells me not to watch it so often, but I can't stop."

"Me too," I exclaimed. "I mean I watch it over and over again. I can't stop!"

"My favorite is the original one with the character Lenny. I loved him," she said.

"I like *Special Victims Unit* the most," I said.

"As a matter of fact," Rene said, "I was just watching an episode of *SVU* before this flight. It's the one about Olivia helping the young woman who is arrested for child neglect."

"I know that one. I always cry. Olivia looks so vulnerable when she holds that baby. I don't care if the plot line is realistic. I love that episode," I responded. "I worry so much that something will happen to the baby. The whole situation seems so precarious and so dear. What's the baby's name?" I asked.

Before she could answer, the pilot announced that the plane would be landing shortly.

After the plane had landed and all of the passengers disembarked, I went to the galley to say goodbye and thanked both women for their kindness to me. I forgot that we'd only known each other for a few hours. We hugged, and then Rene hugged me again.

"We're glad you're here," Rene said.

"I am too. I am too."

✶ ✶ ✶

May Sarton wrote:

> *I felt pain like an assault,*
> *The old pain again*
> *When the world thrusts itself inside,*
> *When we have to take in the outside,*
> *When we have to decide*
> *To be the crazy-human with hope*

Or just plain crazy
With fear.

I think about the fractions of a second that likely made the difference between life and death. What if the beating had lasted another second and injured another portion of my brain? Or caused more damage to the frontal lobe? What if I hadn't kicked or moved or had stopped moving sooner than I did? What if the person who called 911 had waited a few minutes longer before making the call? Or if it had taken the ambulance a few more minutes to get to me? Or a few more minutes to get to the hospital? What if?

Life can change in the blink of an eye, a fraction of a second. I went to Washington filled with hopes and plans. I didn't realize then that hope was a choice.

Now I will make the choice "to be the crazy human with hope."

Hope means thinking about the colors of tulips bulbs I'll plant in the fall that will bloom in the spring. It means allowing myself to dream about traveling and then making plane reservations. Hope means telling old friends that I'll see them at our high school reunion next year. It means watching the news, reading the newspaper, following current event blogs, and talking with friends about domestic and international issues.

Hope means staying awake and aware of the suffering of others, whether stranger or friend.

To choose hope is to let go of my tight grip on the past, to believe in a tomorrow, and risk living, right now. Choosing hope is like doing a trust fall: letting go, trusting that you will be safely caught.

I, of course, did not choose to be attacked, and I had no control over and minimal awareness of many of the falls, literal and figurative, that have happened in its wake. I have been buoyed, braced, and sustained by so many people and by whatever survival nodes live in my DNA helix. Perhaps, most importantly, I have a life that has always been nurtured with love. Love is beyond the reach of hammers and hostility. Love does not obliterate what happened, but it is a salve that can reach under scar tissue, accompany nightmares, and silence the noise of fear. Love is the springboard that allows me to hope.

My story is now yours to feel and share.

Appendix: Suggestions

I t is not easy to know the right thing or best thing to do for someone who has been the victim of random violence, or who lives with
traumatic brain injury and struggles with PTSD. Here are some suggestions from my own experience which may be helpful.

Don't focus only on someone's appearance. For example, saying,
"You look good" or "You've lost weight" or "You've filled out" only
draws attention to the physical body. With PTSD and TBI the most
severe injuries are often invisible. Comments about external appearance can be heard as minimizing the full extent of a person's injury.

You can say something like, "I'm so relieved to see you outside again,"
or "That color looks great on you," or "I don't know what you've been
dealing with, but I think of you all the time and it's so great to share
a laugh with you." These comments move from being overly general
to ones that refer specifically to the person and include your feelings
as well.

Ask real questions about life. "How's work?" Or "How is your
family?" Or "Did you see the game last night?" Or "Did you hear
that Sally Ann just had twins?" Even if your question doesn't lead to
a conversation, it invites the person into the present and underscores
that she/he continues to be a part of a wider community.

It's never too late to say "I'm sorry about what happened." Whether a month or a year has passed, it is not too late to acknowledge your concern and say that the person is in your thoughts. It is better to acknowledge discomfort over not knowing what to say or embarrassment about waiting a long time to offer comments instead of letting something like a life-altering injury go unspoken.

Being uncomfortable or awkward is completely understandable. There is no "exactly right" response to a terrible event and injury. Connection and authenticity are essential and, while sooner is preferable to later, there is no time limit on genuineness. You can say, "I felt so awkward and didn't know what to say and now I feel worse because so much time has passed. I'm always thinking about you and was devastated to hear about . . ."

Don't ask for a rehash of a trauma. If someone wants to tell you about what happened, she/he will give you a signal or start talking. Don't ask, "Do you mind telling me what happened?" The question itself elicits emotional attention to the trauma. And if you do ask for details about what happened and notice hesitation or discomfort, you can say, "I'm sorry for the question. I don't need to know anything except how you are feeling." You can offer a general invitation to talk such as, "If you feel like talking sometime, I'd love to listen."

To be curious and to want to know more are natural responses. Each person moves through a recovery process in a different way and at a different rate. In the very early stages, it is preferable for someone with TBI and PTSD to review, rehash, and relive an event in the presence of trained professionals. The experience of reliving can be highly re-traumatizing. Five years after the assault, I am able to give a brief synopsis of what happened and then stop, or say that I don't want to say anything. Who asks, how the question is posed, and the reasons for the questions all impact my feelings about revealing some details. Reflect on your own motivation for asking questions.

Try not to fill in a word that seems odd or out of place to you when talking with someone who has TBI (or other cognitive impairments), especially if you know the meaning of what is being said. Respond and continue with the conversation. If you don't understand you can say, as you would if you didn't hear someone, "I'm sorry, could you repeat that or tell me again?" If the person is struggling you can paraphrase and say, "Oh, you mean like . . ." It is humiliating to be corrected, such as when the word "cup" is used and the speaker meant "saucer." There is already such a strong feeling of shame when faced with cognitive loss.

"I'm sorry" or "Pardon me" is appropriate in so many situations. If you fill in a word or finish a sentence when someone is hesitating, you can say, "I'm sorry for interrupting. I do that so often." Or, "That was rude, I'm so sorry." Acknowledging what is happening in the moment and taking responsibility for your own actions helps to tamp down the embarrassment.

Traumatic Brain Injury results in permanent losses that may or may not be apparent to you. These losses are, however, a constant source of connection to the incident for the person with TBI. Many people forget a word or use the wrong word in a sentence, especially as a result of the aging process. Those of us with TBI, however, are hypervigilant about making a language mistake and see every mistake as a symptom of TBI and a public demonstration of declining mental acuity.

Try not to deny the reality of TBI by saying, "You sound great," or "I forget words all the time too. Don't worry." You can say, "It's hard to tell that there are any changes. Tell me about what you experience."

Provide space and time for someone with PTSD or TBI to respond to you or to make contact with you. You may call, text, email, Facebook, or Twitter and not get a response. Call and connect anyway. Please don't, however, make the contact if your feelings will be hurt if you don't hear back in what you consider a timely manner. The lack of a suitably timed response may have nothing to do with you, your relationship to the person, or the content of your message. For me, even responding to emails can at different periods feel like an overwhelming responsibility. If I think I'm being judged by how quickly I respond, my stress level rises. You can say in your message, "Thinking of you and just saying hello," or "I wanted to let you know about Marge," or "I want to invite you to . . ." You don't have to respond at all, or you can get in touch whenever it works for you.

Not every reaction is about the trauma or brain injury. Someone may not want to attend a dinner party or take a trip. Try not to problematize each interaction. If an invitation is declined, don't say, "Oh, is it your PTSD? Oh me. Well, we all understand." Let the person offer a reason or simply decline.

Be mindful of sounds, including the sound of your voice. Try not to shout or play music loudly. If you are playing music, ask if the volume is too high. Try to pay attention to how an environment might impact someone with TBI and make modifications, such as lowering the volume and providing for quiet seating arrangements. It is always appropriate to ask if a setting is comfortable. "Is there anything I can do to make you more comfortable?" Once you've asked this question and done whatever possible, don't dwell on the injury or TBI with repeated check-ins or meaningful looks. If you are asked to dim some lights or lower the volume of music, don't see this as your personal failure. Comply if you can and move along.

Time does not erase PTSD or TBI. Time can diminish the intensity of responses or feelings, but it does not eliminate the impact of whatever happened. Try not to ask, "Are you all better?" The implication that something happened and is now all over is not accurate, and the comment is difficult to handle. There is a kind of seesaw between remaining aware of what happened and moving beyond the event lingering at center stage. "How are you doing? It's great to see you so active or relaxed or writing or playing chess," are comments that acknowledge something did happen and allow movement toward something else.

Events like the one I experienced impact so many people. My experience to date is that it also affects everyone who hears about it. You can talk about your own feelings when hearing about a terrible event. You can ask about members of the person's family or friendship circle. And then you can ask again in a month, or a year, or in five years.

Acknowledgments

I must apologize to those whose names I have neglected to mention. This omission is not about your generosity but about my memory. And thank you to all of the kind-hearted people whose names I don't know, who put platters of food on our doorstep, stopped to ask about my health, had the children in your classroom send me get-well cards, offered rides when you saw me walking, and sent get-well cards to someone you had never met. Such kindness is always comforting.

I was cared for by many incredible health professionals. Each was competent and compassionate. They saved my life and my restored my spirit.

Dr. Marianna Marguglio, my primary care physician. You called George Washington Hospital, your alma mater, the moment you heard about the assault to make sure I was getting the best treatment, and you remained my vigilant protector in the years that followed.

Dr. Donald Shields, the neurosurgeon at George Washington University Hospital who likely saved my life. I don't remember you in those first hours and days, but the kindness and assurance I found in your voice remain with me every day.

The trauma team at GW hospital. I don't recall faces, but I do remember the frequent visits of a team of specialists. I didn't have the opportunity to thank you each in person.

Dr. David Refermat, plastic surgeon at Bay State Hospital. I can type this because your gifted hands repaired my broken hands. You treated me with respect and tenderness from the moment I met you. I am grateful for your skills and your decency.

Julie, my occupational therapist. Slowly you brought my hands and many parts of me back to life, and we forged a bond that I continue to cherish.

Dr. Rachel Jenkins, my therapist. I can't find a thank you big enough to encompass how masterfully and lovingly you guided me and led me to knowing what balance felt like. You are a gift beyond measure.

Hasty Hickok, our couples' therapist. Thank you for helping both Debby and me during all of the harrowing times to stay strong and to understand that the assault shattered each of us in different ways, but that it did not shatter our love.

Dr. Ellen Burbrick, neurologist at Brigham and Women's Hospital and faculty member at Harvard University. The seizure brought me to you and I am forever grateful for your guidance, concern, and graciousness.

Dr. Zeina El Chemali, neuro-psychiatrist at Massachusetts General Hospital. Terrible things do happen, but in the midst of my trauma and brain dysregulation, I found you. Thank you for guiding me toward healing, helping me to understand what happened to my brain, and teaching me how to have agency over my own healing.

I am indebted to the many people who read draft after draft after draft of this manuscript: Arlene Avakian, Catherine Baker, Lois Bass, Ange DiBenedetto, Jane Fleishman, Linda Franklin, Perlyn Goodman Herrick, Hilary Jacob Hendel, Karen Hansen, Lisa Herrick, Ari Issler, Marion Jordan, Martha Jordan, Jay Kidd, Nomi Leszkiewicz, Ken Lustbader, Deborah Howland Murray, Jane O'Leary, Hal Offen, Lisa Schnall, Eli Silver, Roz Spafford, Jesse Stoner, Joan Tabachnik, and Gail Weber.

My manuscript group: Kyra Anderson, Katy Drum, Jeanne Fenton, Ashley Fogle, and Dinah Mack. Thank you for reading my chaotic first attempts and being with me as I learned to tell this story by hearing your voices.

Giant applause for Dori Ostermiller, our manuscript leader and teacher extraordinaire, my editor and cheerleader. I could not have completed this book without your guidance.

Many, many people provided essential support from the moment news of the assault was known. Food, rides, visits, shopping, calls to credit card companies, doctors, lawyers. I am in your debt.

Bonnie Allen, Arlene Avakian, Martha Ayres, Steven Botkin, Maria Colella, Judy Davis, Camille Elliott, Mary Elizabeth Fahey, Kate Fahey, Carol Gray, Georganne Greene, Pat Griffin, Karen Hansen, Bobbie Harro, Bertha Josephson, Andrea Kendal, Jay Kidd, Margaret Kirstein, Connie Kruger, Joan Levy, Ken Lustbader, Jane Mildred, Susan Tracy, Val Young, and Ximena Zuniga.

Pat Romney and Linda Marchesani, thank you for knowing that you needed to be in D.C. with me, Debby, and Rachel, and then just coming. Who does that? Mensches do.

Sheila O'Brien and Kevin Peterson. In addition to your deep and abiding love, you provided what I didn't know I needed and made it possible for me to return home safely.

I am blessed with a family whose devotion and unconditional love I have always known.

My parents, Evelyn Silver and Ben Silver. You gave me the riches of a strong and sturdy foundation and a clear moral compass. Time does not lessen how much I miss you.

Mary Silver, my sister-in-law. You flew, without hesitation, to Massachusetts, rented a car, drove to Amherst in order to drive both of us to Boston the next day, and accompanied me on my first trip to California after the assault.

Martha Jordon, Joel Silver, Sheila O'Brien, your visits buoyed my spirits immeasurably. I didn't realize how your visits would also include fixing things, gardening, cooking, shopping for what we needed, organizing, helping me to regain the confidence to leave the house, and re-teaching me how to tie my shoes.

Eli Silver, my older brother. You've always been there for me, without question and without hesitation. The assault exceeded the bounds of sibling support, and I drew on your love and strength, as I have all of my life.

My step-son, Robbie. The image of you squeezing your six-foot, five-inch frame onto a small bike to get to our house the night of my seizure is seared into my heart. Thank you for your constant love for me.

Savi, my beloved grandson. I'm so sorry that the assault and its aftermath has taken up such a big part of your childhood. You are a beacon of courage for me.

Rachel, my dearest, dearest daughter. I would do anything to erase memories of me after the assault, and all of the tumult that has followed. Your love has sustained me through the worst of this experience and continues to give me boundless joy and strength every day.

Debby, my wife, my best friend, my caretaker, my companion, my heart. I could not have done this—heal, find ways to move forward, and live with the daily consequences—without you. Can I have this dance for the rest of my life?

About the Author

Dr. JoAnne Silver Jones is Professor Emeritus from Springfield College, Springfield, Massachusetts, where she was a professor and associate dean for twenty-five years. Prior to Springfield College, she was an associate professor at the University of Massachusetts, Amherst and an assistant professor of social welfare at the University of Calgary, School of Social Welfare. Her teaching and research focused primarily on social justice issues.

Her teaching and writing was recognized in North America and Northern Europe where, in Sweden, she introduced a master of science degree designed for adult learners.

The assault that is at the heart of her first book, *Headstrong: Surviving Traumatic Brain Injury*, reshaped her life. Her passion for justice was, if anything, emboldened as she immersed herself in understanding traumatic brain injury, post-traumatic stress syndrome, the consequence of being the victim of stranger violence, the cultural contexts and blocks to recovery, and the ways in which trauma pervades daily life.

SELECTED TITLES FROM SHE WRITES PRESS

She Writes Press is an independent publishing company founded to serve women writers everywhere. Visit us at www.shewritespress.com.

But My Brain Had Other Ideas: A Memoir of Recovery from Brain Injury by Deb Brandon $16.95, 978-1631522468
When Deb Brandon discovered that cavernous angiomas—tangles of malformed blood vessels in her brain—were what was behind her the terrifying symptoms she'd been experiencing, she underwent one brain surgery. And then another. And then another. And that was just the beginning.

Room 23: Surviving a Brain Hemorrhage by Kavita Basi $16.95, 978-1-63152-489-9
Kavita Basi had a seemingly perfect world—a nice job, excellent holidays, strong family bonds—until she was diagnosed with subarachnoid hemorrhage, a serious illness with a 50 percent mortality rate, and everything changed.

A Leg to Stand On: An Amputee's Walk into Motherhood by Colleen Haggerty $16.95, 978-1-63152-923-8
Haggerty's candid story of how she overcame the pain of losing a leg at seventeen—and of terminating two pregnancies as a young woman—and went on to become a mother, despite her fears.

Second Chance: A Mother's Quest for a Natural Birth after a Cesarean by Thais Derich $16.95, 978-1-63152-218-5
Traumatized by an unwanted cesarean, Derich begins the long journey toward learning to trust herself so she can go against societal norms and give birth to her second child the way she wants: naturally, and at home.

Painting Life: My Creative Journey Through Trauma by Carol K. Walsh $16.95, 978-1-63152-099-0
Carol Walsh was a psychotherapist working with traumatized clients when she encountered her own traumatic experience; this is the story of how she used creativity and artistic expression to heal, recreate her life, and ultimately thrive.